Strategies *for* College Success

A Study Skills Guide

Diana Renn

Boston University

University of Michigan Press
Ann Arbor

Acknowledgments

I want to thank Kelly Sippell, senior ESL acquisitions editor at the University of Michigan Press, for starting me on the path of writing this book and for her encouragement along the way. I would also like to thank everyone at the University of Michigan Press who participated in this project's development. I would like to thank the colleagues I've been privileged to work with, who reviewed early stages of this manuscript or provided inspiration and advice along the way. Among them are Martha Hauston, Gloria Monaghan, Diane Sweet, David Spenard, and Dr. Allyson McCabe. I wish to thank Dr. Barbara Karanian and the librarians at Wentworth Institute of Technology for assisting with reading materials. In addition, I must thank the Writer's Room of Boston for providing a quiet sanctuary in which to work.

I extend a heartfelt thanks to my family and their ongoing enthusiasm for my work. I am especially grateful to my beloved husband Jim, who was supportive of my long hours in front of the computer even as we embarked on a new life together. His patience, encouragement, good humor, and excellent meals sustained me through the writing of this book.

Grateful acknowledgment is made to the following authors, publishers, and organizations for permission to reprint previously published materials.

Heldref Publications for "Relationship of Sleep Hygiene Awareness, Sleep Hygiene Practices, and Sleep Quality in University Students" by Franklin C. Brown, Walter C. Buboltz, Jr., and Barlow Soper, in *Behavioral Medicine*, Spring 2002, vol. 28, issue 1. Reprinted with permission of the Helen Dwight Reid Educational Foundation. Published by Heldref Publications, 1319 18th Street NW, Washington, DC 20036-1802. *www.heldref.org*. Copyright © 2002.

Manisses Communications Group, Inc. for "A Professor's Crash Course Is College Student's Dream: A Class on the Importance of Sleep" from *The Brown University Child and Adolescent Behavior Letter*, April 1997. Reprinted with permission of Manisses Communications Group, Inc.

Ji Yun Park for "Education of Korea vs. U.S.A."

Pearson Education, Inc. for material from *Web Wizard's Guide to Web Design*, pp. 18–27, by James G. Lengel. Copyright © 2002 Pearson Education. Reprinted by permission of Pearson Education, Inc. Publishing as Pearson Addison Wesley.

Penguin Group (USA) Inc. for an excerpt from *I Don't Know What I Want, but I Know It's Not This: A Step-by-Step Guide to Finding Gratifying Work* by Julie Jansen. Copyright © 2003 by Julie Jansen. Used by permission of Penguin, a division of Penguin Group (USA) Inc.

Project Innovation for "Multiple Intelligences in the Classroom: Characteristics of the Eight Types of Intelligences as Identified by Howard Gardner" by Jennifer L. Nolen, from *Education,* Fall 2003. Reprinted with permission of Project Innovation.

Shambhala Publications, Inc. for an excerpt from *The Lotus and the Pool* by Hilda Lee Dail. Copyright © 1983. Reprinted by arrangement with Shambhala Publications, Inc., Boston, *www.shambhala.com.*

South-Western, for an excerpt from *Principles of Microeconomics, 3rd Edition,* by N. Gregory Mankiw. Copyright © 2004. Reprinted with permission of South-Western, a division of Thomson Learning: *www.thomsonrights.com.* Fax 800-730-2215.

Katira Tejeda for "Grandmother's Backyard" and "Americans Work."

Chiharu Tomihara for "Japanese Speech."

Wadsworth for excerpts from *Sociology: A Global Perspective (with InfoTrac), 5th edition,* by Joan Ferrante. Copyright © 2003. Reprinted with permission of Wadsworth, a division of Thomson Learning: *www.thomsonrights.com.* Fax 800-730-2215.

Western Michigan University for "Expert Says Popular Time Management Techniques Won't Work for All" by Jessica English, from the *WMU News,* June 14, 2000.

John Wiley & Sons for Learning Styles Self-Assessment Chart from *Learn More Now: 10 Simple Steps to Learning Better, Smarter, and Faster* by Marcia L. Connor. Copyright © 2004. Reprinted with permission of John Wiley & Sons, Inc.

Zon Zon Win for sample journal entries and a grammar log.

Kin Wong for "*Typical American* and the American Dream."

Corbis, for the following photos: Running Out of Time, Girl Reading Book in Library, Family Serving a Meal at a Shelter, Young Woman Using Cell Phone while Eating, People Using Stationary Bikes, Sleeping in Class, Colleagues in a Meeting.

Every effort has been made to contact the copyright holders for permission to reprint borrowed material. We regret any oversights that may have occurred and will rectify them in future printings of this book.

Contents

Part 1: Study Skills

1   TIME   3

4 INNOVATIONS · 91

5 HEALTH · 121

List of Strategies, by Chapter

List of Strategies, by Type

List of Study Tips and Writing Tips, by Chapter

To the Teacher

Introduction

Strategies for College Success is an academic study skills book primarily for English language learners who are planning to attend an American college or who may already be enrolled in their first year of a community college or a four-year college. The book may also be used for college success seminars for first-year students; native or near-native English speakers needing a stronger foundation for college success can benefit from the skills and strategies presented here. The book introduces all students to the language and culture of college.

    Strategies for College Success may be used as a text for a general study skills class or as a supplementary text for a class with a writing focus. Though the book emphasizes communication skills for group situations and many of the activities are designed with groups in mind, the book can also be used for self-study.

    The main goal of this text is to encourage students to become self-directed learners and better participants in an academic community. Students need strong academic skills in order to thrive in college classes alongside native English speakers or more conventionally prepared college students. However, information about the expectations and the "culture" of college is also important. Students often experience a kind of "culture shock" when they get to college, whether or not they are from another country. Therefore, this book combines academic study skills with activities and information designed to help students adjust to other aspects of North American college life. Students who use this book will gain confidence in expressing their ideas both orally and in writing. They will have the confidence to approach a wide variety of assignments and communicative tasks awaiting them in their first year of college and beyond. Finally, they will learn what rights and responsibilities they have as members of an academic community, thereby empowering themselves to become active learners and get the most out of their college experience.

Key Features

Some of the key features of this book are as follows:

- **An integrated skills approach** helps students face a wide range of communicative tasks, including participating in class and small group discussions, delivering oral presentations, approaching various types of writing assignments, recognizing different types of test questions, taking and organizing lecture notes, creating graphic organizers, and improving reading proficiency.

- **Authentic, cross-curricular readings** include brief selections from textbooks currently used in North American college courses, as well as articles from magazines, newspapers, and journals of academic interest. The reading content represents academic disciplines within the broad categories of Humanities, Sciences, Social Sciences, and Business. The cross-curricular subject matter also introduces students to the concept of academic disciplines and the habit of evaluating different types of sources.

- **An audio component with academic lectures** gives students the opportunity to practice listening to academic lectures and taking notes. The lectures relate to the theme of each chapter. They also represent content and vocabulary from a variety of academic disciplines: anthropology, psychology, sociology, philosophy/ethics, and American history/American studies. The listening component of this book may also help students prepare for the listening section on the Next Generation TOEFL® test. An audio compact disk is available.

- **Carefully sequenced questions, activities, and writing prompts** following readings and lectures guide students through the processes of comprehension, critical thinking, inference, and analysis that first-year college students must be able to engage in.

- **A combination of individual and collaborative activities** encourages students both to think independently and to work with a group. Speaking skills are emphasized to reduce anxiety commonly associated with class discussions and oral presentations. Students will be prepared to succeed in classes that have a strong "class participation" component.

- **Writing activities of varying lengths and levels of difficulty** allow instructors to use this text in mixed-ability classrooms. Writing tasks can be modified to meet the needs of their classes or of individual students. Cross-references to a separate writing section allow instructors to implement a writing focus if they choose.

- **Graphics strategies** sections provide practice with graphic literacy. Students interpret data in commonly used graphic organizers. They also create their own graphs with information related to the chapter theme.
- **"Orientation" sections** introduce students to important resources in an academic community. Students learn about resources such as Campus Learning Centers, Health and Counseling Services, and Career Services. Students can visit local colleges, explore their current academic community, or research colleges online to locate these various resources for themselves.
- **Test-taking strategies** expose students to the main types of test questions they will encounter: multiple choice, short answer, essay questions, and timed essays. Practice test items allow students to apply the test-taking strategy to the content they have learned in the chapter. Additional chapter tests can be found on the website companion to this text.
- **Check Your Progress** self-assessment charts and questions raise students' awareness of their own learning style and processes. They also inform the instructor about what material might need to be reviewed.
- **Study tips** occur throughout the book. Approximately five tips per chapter appear in boxes. Students can be encouraged to try these tips on their own and report—orally or in a journal—how and when they applied these tips.

How to Use This Book

Part 1, which uses an integrated skills approach, presents learning strategies in six chapters. Each content-based chapter focuses on a different theme: *Time, Learning, Communities, Innovations, Health,* and *Work.* The broad themes allow ample opportunity for students to connect their own life experiences and academic interests to the readings and lectures. For students who have not yet determined a focus of academic interest, the exposure to readings and ideas from different disciplines may spark interest in pursuing a particular area of study in college or at least taking a class in that subject.

Part 2, which focuses on writing issues, contains two chapters. While this book does not go into as much detail about writing compared with texts that are focused on writing skills, it does present an overview of the writing process, paragraph format, and essay format. Part 2 can be used in conjunction with the chapters in Part 1; writing tasks in Part 1 are cross-referenced with appropriate sections in Part 2.

Each chapter in Part 1 uses the same format:

- **Warm-Up.** Activities are designed to get students thinking and talking about the chapter theme. Chapter openers take the form of individual questionnaires, ranking activities, classroom surveys, and discussion questions. Students can discuss their responses in small groups and/or write them as informal journal entries.

- **Key Words.** Ten key vocabulary words for the chapter are presented, and a practice activity is provided. Students may encounter these key words in various chapter activities, the chapter reading, and the chapter listening activity. Instructors may wish to quiz students on the key words periodically if they desire more emphasis on vocabulary. *Students should use an English-English dictionary for the vocabulary exercises.*

- **Vocabulary Strategies.** One or two vocabulary strategies are presented in each chapter. The strategies are reviewed and recycled in subsequent chapters.

- **Speaking Strategy.** Each section presents a strategy for oral communication, from participating in discussions to giving a presentation. Students should consciously apply the strategy at some point during a discussion or class, and account for it in the self-assessment chart at the end of the chapter.

- **Reading Strategy.** One or two reading strategies are presented in each chapter. The strategies are then applied to the chapter reading. Reading strategies are reviewed and recycled in subsequent chapters. Additionally, instructors may wish to provide additional readings related to the chapter themes and have students apply the reading strategies to them.

- **Chapter Readings.** Each chapter contains a selection from an authentic college textbook, an academic article, or a magazine or news article of academic interest. More advanced classes could be encouraged to read—or find—additional readings related to the topics. The reading selections for this text are of varying lengths. Some chapter readings are relatively short, yet they may have more challenging vocabulary or content compared to some of the longer readings. In addition to the chapter readings, very short readings (one to five paragraphs) are provided in the vocabulary section of each chapter. While these readings may be used for discussion or writing activities, their primary purpose is to help students apply the vocabulary strategies. Finally, in-text citations and footnotes from the original articles have been removed so that students can focus on the content and on reading/vocabulary strategies.

- **Academic Listening Strategies.** Each chapter includes one or more listening strategies to help students take effective notes and listen for certain types of information. Students can then listen to the lectures on the audio component that accompanies this text and apply the listening strategies. Alternatively, the instructor may read the lectures aloud from the transcripts in the back of the book.

- **Academic Lectures.** The lectures recorded on the audio component represent various academic disciplines and topics. While they are not authentic lectures from college classes, they are written to expose students to some of the language associated with these disciplines at the college level. The pace of these lectures is slightly slower than it would be in an actual college classroom. This slower pace is designed to help students practice listening for important information and taking notes. Examples of good student notes are provided in the appendix, and students should be encouraged to compare their results.

- **Writing Strategies**. One or more writing strategies are presented in each chapter. This section may be supplemented with appropriate pages in Part 2 or with an additional writing text or handbook. Models of student writing for various writing tasks are included in the cross-referenced writing section. However, these writing samples have been corrected and modified. It is important to reassure students that the *sample student works do not represent first drafts.*

- **Writing Task**. For each task there is a choice of topics for paragraphs or essays related to the chapter theme. Instructors should consider the level of the class or the needs of their students in determining whether to assign paragraphs or essays. The topic choices also help instructors to accommodate mixed-ability classes. Topic 1 is suitable for lower-level writers, Topic 2 for intermediate writers, and Topic 3 for more advanced writers. More advanced students should be encouraged to write full-length essays and to choose the third topic choice. Beginning writers could be asked to write paragraphs. Alternatively, a class with a strong writing component might start with paragraph-length assignments and Topic 1 choices, working up to essay-length assignments and Topic 3 choices by the end of the course. Finally, regardless of the level of writers, peer review should be encouraged; students can read each other's drafts and respond to them with the aid of a checklist of key points to look for. These checklists can also be used for students to check their own work on a subsequent revision. See pages 225–27.

- **Graphics Strategy.** Information related to the chapter theme, to the chapter reading, or to some aspect of college life is presented in the form of a graphic organizer. Students will learn strategies for interpreting graphs as well as for creating their own. Students can be encouraged to create graphic organizers to help them understand what they read, to consider ideas for a writing assignment, or to use as part of their final project in each chapter.

- **Test-Taking Strategy**. Each chapter includes a test-taking strategy and demonstrates the process of working through different types of test items. Students can then practice the strategy with several additional test questions. More chapter tests, which can be used to assess students' mastery of the content of each chapter, can be found on the companion website for this book. See *www.press.umich.edu/esl/*.

- **Orientation.** This section introduces students to various aspects of college life, such as campus resources and officials. The Orientation activities ask students to explore the resources at their existing school or to research them at a local college or online. The activities may be expanded to allow for more formal group presentations or for additional writing practice.

- **Final Project.** Each chapter concludes with options for a written and/or oral project. These final projects can be omitted, used selectively, modified, or expanded, at the instructor's discretion. The final project options ask students to take the theme of the chapter outside the classroom in some way, perhaps by conducting field research (surveying American students on a topic related to the readings or lectures or observing and taking notes somewhere) or by conducting relevant Internet or library research. Students can then present the information in the form of an essay, a report, or an oral presentation. Final projects can be individual or collaborative. The flexibility of the final project topics allows instructors to tailor these projects to the needs of their classes.

- **Check Your Progress.** Students should use the assessment charts and questions to evaluate how well they feel they have understood and applied the skills presented in the chapter, and to identify what they should continue to work on.

Pacing

Strategies for College Success is adaptable to different types of courses. For semester-long programs (12–14 weeks), instructors may wish to spend approximately two weeks on each chapter. For programs of fewer than 12 weeks, instructors might only teach selected chapters. If instructors are unable to cover the entire text in a course, they can omit some of the tasks or the final projects; they may also assign some of the tasks as homework rather than as in-class activities. For a two-semester course, instructors can have students do most of the tasks in class. They can also encourage the development of reading and writing skills by supplementing this text with additional readings and writing activities. Instructors might also encourage expansion activities and completion of all the final projects.

To the Student

Congratulations! If you are reading this book, you have probably entered a college program, you are preparing to enter a college program, or you are thinking about entering a college program. In any case, you are making an important decision: to continue your education at a higher level. You may be training for a specific career, or you may want to get a higher degree so that you have more choices in the job market. Whatever your reasons, and wherever you are, you should be very proud of how far you have come in your education. This is especially true if English is not your native language. Not everyone can understand another language well enough to use it at the college level. If you have come this far in your education, you are already successful!

You should also realize that your journey isn't over yet. In fact, it is just beginning. College is very different from high school. The work is harder, and there is more of it. The speed is different; more material is covered in less time. And in large classes, professors may not notice if you need additional help. It will be entirely your responsibility to make sure you are keeping up with assignments and understanding the material. Your success in college depends mostly on you.

You may have attended high school—or even taken college classes—in a different country. If you have, this book will help you to understand how North American classrooms and assignments may be a little different from what you are used to. For example, some people are surprised that professors expect students to speak a lot in class, and to discuss their opinions. Some people don't realize that the structure of essays and paragraphs may be different from what is used in other countries. (For example, do you state the main idea of an essay at the beginning or at the end?) Some people don't understand the types of comments that professors may write on their papers, or the requirements of different types of assignments. *Strategies for College Success* helps you to recognize the most common types of assignments and activities that you will find in first-year college classes.

In addition, this book will help you to learn important study skills that will help you to do well in your college classes. You will learn strategies for improving your reading, writing, listening, and speaking. You will learn how to take good notes from readings and from lectures, how to take tests, and how to study. You will also gain an understanding of your personal learning style, and the study strategies that work best for *you*.

College isn't only about the material that you learn from your textbooks and lectures. A lot of learning in college takes place outside the classroom. When you make a decision to enter a college, you become part of a community—an *academic community*. As a member of this community, you suddenly have access to a lot of information and many resources. This book will introduce you to a few of those resources. You will also learn about how to communicate with your professors, where to find help if you need it, and how you can plan your time. Most important, you will learn about *the language and culture of college.*

After reading this book and practicing the strategies, you should know what to expect in a North American college classroom. You should recognize and have practiced some common types of assignments and activities. Above all, you should feel more confident in your ability to succeed in your classes and to participate in an academic community.

Getting Started

Getting to Know Your Textbook

The first thing you should do when you start a new class is to get to know your textbook. What are you going to learn? Where can you find certain kinds of information? How easy or difficult does the material seem to be?

Find the following parts of this textbook.

1. The **Contents** (sometimes called Table of Contents) tell you what kind of information is in the book. It tells you the chapters and page numbers where you can find that information.

    a. How many parts does this book have? _____

    b. How many chapters does this book have? _____

    c. What is the main subject of each chapter in Part I?

    _____

    _____

    d. On what page can you find an article called "Expert Says Popular Time Management Techniques Won't Work for All?" _____

    e. On what page can you find information on Creating Pie Charts? _____

    f. On what page can you find information on keeping a Grammar/Error Log?_____

2. An **Appendix** (plural: *appendices or appendixes*) contains additional information related to the chapter. Sometimes charts, tables, or certain kinds of forms are given in this section of a book. Use the Contents to find the appendix (or appendices) of this book.

    List three things you can find in the Appendix of this book:

    _____

    _____

3. Look through the chapters in Part 1.

    Which chapter looks most interesting to you? _____

    Why? _____

    _____

Getting Organized

It's important to have the right supplies to help you to organize your work. Here are some things that you may need to buy at the beginning of a new class or semester. Put a check mark by the things that you already have. If you are not sure what some of these supplies are or where to find them, ask your instructor or another student in your class.

- ☐ Three-ring notebook
- ☐ Dividers for your notebook (You can put your notes and handouts for each class in your notebook and separate them with dividers, or buy a separate three-ring notebook for each class.)
- ☐ A three-hole punch
- ☐ Lined paper
- ☐ Pens and pencils
- ☐ Highlighter pens in different colors
- ☐ Computer disks (or zip disks)
- ☐ A stapler and staples, or paperclips
- ☐ A sturdy backpack or bookbag

Setting Personal Learning Goals

At the beginning of a new class, think about your strengths (things you are good at), your weaknesses (things you need to improve), and your goals (what you want to learn in the class). It's useful to write these down and to look back on them from time to time. Try to think of at least three items for each category.

For example, a student using this book for a class might write the following:

My strengths: I am good at coming up with ideas for writing assignments, correcting grammar mistakes in my writing, and taking tests.

My weaknesses: It is hard for me to speak in class. I don't usually ask questions or ask a teacher for help when I don't understand something. I sometimes don't remember what I read.

My goals: My main goals in this class are to speak more in class discussions, to talk to the professor or other students when I need help, and to improve my reading comprehension.

⤳ **PART 1**

Study Skills

1 ❧ Time

1. Read these proverbs, or sayings, about time. What do you think each expression means? Discuss possible meanings with a small group. Give an example of each one from your experience or your observations.

   > *Lost time is never found again.*
   > *Time is money.*
   > *Time flies when you're having fun.*
   > *Make hay while the sun shines.*
   > *Work smarter, not harder.*
   > *The early bird catches the worm.*
   > *Early to bed, early to rise, makes a man healthy, wealthy, and wise.*

2. Do you know other sayings about time? Does your culture have special sayings about time? Does your family? Share them with your group and explain their meaning. Give examples. Are anyone's sayings similar to the ones listed above?

3. Which saying about time best describes how you feel about time? Why?

Key Words

Using a Dictionary

An important tool for college success is a dictionary. A good dictionary will tell you the meaning or meanings of words. It will also give you the different *forms* of a word—that is, it will tell you if the word can be used as a **noun** (a person, place, or thing), a **verb** (an action word), an **adjective** (a word that describes a noun), or an **adverb** (a word that describes a verb or an adjective). Different word forms often have different spellings.

Here is a sample dictionary entry for a word:

the word   how to pronounce the word   word form (here, a verb)   definition

procrastinate /prou'kraeste neit/ *v.* delay action, especially repeatedly: He procrastinated until it was too late. procrastination: *n.*

a different word form (noun)   an example sentence with the word

Now read the words in the box. You will see these key words used in this chapter. Circle any words you don't know. Use a dictionary to check the meanings. Then use the words to complete the sentences.

conflict	flexible	precise	put off	tasks
disorganized	organized	procrastination	simultaneously	time management

1. The job has a _____ schedule. You can choose which days and hours you wish to work, and you can change your schedule if you need to.

2. Professor Spenard is very _____. He always begins his class exactly at 1:00 and ends exactly at 2:20.

3. I can't take Intro to Psychology because there is a time _____ with my math class. Both classes meet on Tuesdays and Thursdays at 2:00.

4. My sister can do many things at once, but I can't do things _____. I work best when I focus only on one thing at a time.

5. Don't _____ doing your homework assignments. Homework done at the last minute may not receive a good grade.

6. I have many _____ to do today, including studying for two quizzes, reviewing my lecture notes, and exercising.

7. In her messy room, Julia has papers all over her desk and notes stuffed into the wrong files. She is very _____. It's no wonder she can never find anything she needs!

8. Buying school supplies like files and folders, as well as keeping your workspace _____, can save you time. If you know where your things are, you won't waste time looking for them.

9. Appointment books, day planners, and computer programs can help people with _____. It's important to find a schedule planning system that works well for *you*.

10. Spending too much time on e-mail or on the Internet can lead to _____. Before you know it, hours can pass by and it will be too late to do your work.

■ Vocabulary Strategies

◎ *Strategy 1A: Deciding Which Words Are Important to Know*

In your college readings and lectures, you will see a lot of new words. Don't worry if you don't understand every word of an article or a textbook chapter.

It's important to look up new words in a dictionary. However, looking up *every* new word can slow down your reading. You should read the text once without looking up words and see how much you understand on your own. Then you can look for important words to check in the dictionary. Here are some questions to ask about each new word:

- Does the word appear in a title, subtitle, or heading?
- Does the word repeat?
- Does the word appear in other word forms? *(procrastinate, procrastination)*
- Does the word appear in the first or last sentence of a paragraph? (These are places where main ideas are usually stated.)
- Does the word appear in *italics* or **boldface**? Is it followed by a definition or explanation?
- Does the word have a synonym nearby? (A synonym is a word with the same or similar meaning.) Often synonyms are connected with *and*.
- Does the word clearly relate to the main idea of the reading? (Does it relate to the title? To a controlling idea stated early in the reading?)

If you answer YES to any of these questions, the word is probably an important word to know. You should look it up in a dictionary to be sure that you understand it. If you answered NO to any of these questions, you might be able to understand the reading without looking up the word.

Be careful of words that begin with CAPITAL LETTERS. They usually name places or people (for example: *Boston College, Mississippi, Steinberg Research Institute*). They are probably not in the dictionary. Also, watch out for words or phrases at the beginning of sentences that introduce information or quotations (for example, *according to, nevertheless*). These words may just be sentence connectors.

PRACTICE

Read this passage from a student newspaper. Decide which of the highlighted words are important and why.

Setting Priorities

An important part of time management is the ability to set priorities for yourself. First, list all the tasks you need to do. Then decide which activities are the most important and the least important. Number them in the order of importance, or put the activities on two lists—one list of very important things and one list of less important things. Another way to think of prioritizing your to-do list is not in terms of importance, but in terms of time. Which tasks must be done immediately? Which tasks can wait? According to Jane Holt, the director of the Learning Center at Shorewood Community College, a mistake that people often make is to first do the most enjoyable tasks on their list. "Then they put off doing the least enjoyable tasks," says Holt. "This is a mistake because doing the fun things makes them feel busy and productive, when in fact they are just procrastinating the tasks that make them uncomfortable." This procrastination can lead to anxiety and stress. As a result, some tasks might never get completed, or they might be done less effectively. Most people can't do an effective job when they're too tired or they don't have enough time. A key to managing time, then, is to list everything you need to do and then to figure out which tasks need your attention first.

Now complete the word chart below. The first one is done for you.

Word	Is It Important?	Why or Why Not?
management	Yes	The word repeats in a different form
priorities		
tasks		
According		
Holt		
Shorewood		
productive		
procrastination		
anxiety		
effectively		

◎ Strategy 1B: Keeping a Vocabulary Log

Building your vocabulary will help you to have more things to say in class discussions and more things to write about in your writing assignments. In addition, a larger vocabulary will help you to understand your readings more quickly. It's important to spend time on your own remembering the new words you learn. A Vocabulary Log can help you to do this.

A *log* is a list that is updated (added to) regularly. You can keep your log in a separate section of your notebook or as a computer file. Choose five new words from a reading or lecture each week. Choose words that are interesting to you and that you want to remember. Write them in a chart like the one on page 9. Pay special attention to word forms. Notice how the word is used in the sentence in which you found it. Be careful to use the correct word form in your own sentence.

Review your Vocabulary Log every week, especially before class discussions and writing assignments. Try to use words from your log in your speaking and your writing.

New Word	Sentence You Found or Heard It In	Word Form (Noun, Verb, Adjective, or Adverb)	Other Word Forms It Can Take	Definition and/or Translation	Use the Word in Your Own Sentence
priorities	An important part of time management is the ability to set priorities for yourself.	noun (plural)	prioritize (verb)	Things that are important to do	My priorities tonight are studying for the test, reading Chapter One, and eating a healthy dinner. Watching TV is not a priority, so I'll do that another day.
tasks	First, list all the tasks you need to do.	noun (plural)	No other word forms	Things to do; jobs or activities to complete	I have many tasks to do tonight, including reviewing for the quiz, studying my vocabulary log, and calling my sister.
procrasti-nation	This procrastination can lead to anxiety and stress.	noun	procrasti-nate (verb)	Putting off or delaying doing something until a later time	My friend always procrastinates doing his homework. Because he does it right before class, he always feels stressed and he doesn't remember what he learns.
effectively	As a result, some tasks might never get completed, or they might be done less effectively.	adverb	effective (adjective)	Well; in a good way; in a way that will give good results	Writing a paper with the TV on is not an effective way to work. You can't work effectively with that noise and distraction.
productive	This is a mistake be-cause doing the fun things makes them feel busy and productive, when in fact they are just procrastinating the tasks that make them uncomfortable.	adjective	produc-tively (adverb); productiv-ity (noun)	In a way that pro-duces a lot of results; effective	My brother has a very productive work style. He is able to read three ar-ticles and write a para-graph in one evening because he works in a quiet place and does not do other activities at the same time.

PRACTICE

Choose five new words from the reading on pages 14–15 of this chapter or from something else that you read this week on your own. Start your Vocabulary Log this week, using this chart. You can copy the chart in Appendix A or create a similar one in your notebook or on a computer.

■ Speaking Strategy

◎ Strategy 1: Understanding "Class Participation"

Some of your classes in college will be **lecture classes**. This means that you will mostly listen to your professor or instructor (these terms are used interchangeably throughout this text) and take notes. However, you will probably have **discussion sections,** or **seminars** (classes with more discussion than lecture), in which you will be expected to talk a lot. "Class participation" is an important part of most American college classes. It might be worth 10 percent of your grade or more!

You may be surprised to learn that professors want to know your opinion. You may hear students disagreeing with one another in a discussion. Students might even challenge or disagree with things that their professors say!

Talking in class isn't easy for everyone. Sometimes people aren't sure about their ideas. Some people prefer to listen to others. Some people don't feel confident about speaking in English. These concerns are normal. However, when you are graded on class participation, it's important to make efforts to improve in this area.

✓ Ten Tips for Speaking in Class

1. Before class, look at the class schedule or the reading. You should know the topic of your next class. Write down some things you might say.

2. Try to say something early in the class discussion. The longer you wait, the more anxiety you may have about speaking.

3. Make it your goal to say at least one thing in each class. Then work up to two things in the next class, then three, and so on. Keep track of how many times you speak in each class. (However, speak thoughtfully—be sure that your questions or comments relate to the topic and add to the discussion in some way.)

4. Give yourself rewards for speaking. For example: "I spoke three times in the last class discussion. If I speak six times today, I'll buy myself a new CD."

5. Take advantage of opportunities to participate in small ways. You could volunteer to read something aloud in class. This counts as class participation and is a good way to get used to hearing your voice in a classroom.

6. If the professor puts you into small groups for discussions, say as much as you can. It's easier to speak in a small group, and you'll gain confidence hearing yourself talk. Also, the professor will probably notice if you are normally quiet in large group discussion but you are making extra effort in a small group.

7. Highlight or underline parts of your text. If you need to refer to something in a discussion, you will be able to find it more quickly. (See Reading Strategy 3, Highlighting and Underlining a Text, in Chapter 3 on page 70.)

8. Ask a question if you don't understand something. It's another way to get used to hearing your voice in the classroom. Also, professors like to know if people don't understand the material. Questions let professors know what they need to review. You are probably not the only one with a question.

9. Remember that you are not alone! Many people feel self-conscious or shy speaking in class when English is not their native language, or when they are not yet sure about their ideas or their vocabulary.

10. Be a good listener when other people are speaking. Assume that other people will listen to you just as carefully.

PRACTICE

Choose at least one class participation tip from the list above. Use this strategy in your class discussions and activities in this chapter.

✓ Study Tip: Plan Your Reading Time

Reading for classes usually takes more time than reading for pleasure. Never read a reading assignment immediately before class. Give yourself time to read it more than once (two or three times is best), to look up important new words, to be sure you understand the main ideas, and to write questions about things you don't understand.

■ Reading Strategy

◎ Strategy 1: SQ3R (Survey, Question, Read, Recite, Review)

Use the SQ3R system each time you read an article or a chapter in a textbook. SQ3R means **S**urvey, **Q**uestion, **R**ead, **R**ecite, **R**eview.

1. Survey

Preview the reading by **skimming** (reading very quickly) or **scanning** (looking for specific features of the text). Specifically, look at the title, as well as any headings or subtitles, charts, and illustrations. Look at the first and last sentences of paragraphs. What will the reading be about? How long is the reading? How long are the paragraphs or sections? Do sentences seem long or short? Do you see a lot of new words? How difficult or easy do you think the reading will be?

PRACTICE

Preview the reading on pages 14–15 of this chapter. What is it probably about?

_____

_____

_____

How difficult does this reading seem to be? Why?

_____

_____

_____

2. Question

Write down questions about the reading. What do you think it will tell you about the topic? Pretend you are a newspaper reporter. Write questions that start with W *(Who? What? When? Where? Why?)* or H *(How?).*

PRACTICE

Write three W or H questions about the reading on pages 14–15. For example: *What are popular time management techniques?*

Question 1: _____

Question 2: _____

Question 3: _____

3. Read

Read once, quickly, to see how much you understand on your own. Look for answers to the questions you wrote. Write down new questions as you read. Then read again. Highlight or circle vocabulary words that you think are important to know. Look up the words and, if you have time, read again.

PRACTICE

Read the article, following the guidelines explained above.

Western Michigan University News

Expert Says Popular Time Management Techniques Won't Work for All

KALAMAZOO—You're feeling guilty.

The expensive day planner that was supposed to revolutionize the way you work is sitting on the corner of your desk gathering dust, practically untouched since your company sent you to that time management course. In fact, the thought of plotting out your days and weeks in such precise increments makes you cringe. Maybe you're just disorganized by nature.

Or perhaps you're a polychron.

A Western Michigan University professor is researching time management styles in the workplace, and his findings could change the way we perceive time and organization. Using a system that categorizes people as "monochronic" or "polychronic" time managers, Dr. Jay D. Lindquist, professor of marketing in the Haworth College of Business, is investigating why and how people use and organize their time. He and Dr. Carol Kaufman-Scarborough of Rutgers University are studying the characteristics associated with both types of time managers, and the duo recently published a portion of their work in the *Journal of Managerial Psychology*.

"We believe a person's time personality is made up of a series of time styles, just as the other researchers believe a person's overall personality is made up of traits," Lindquist says. "We are theorizing that time activity level—be it monochronic, polychronic or balanced—is one of the contributing styles to a person's overall time personality."

Monochronic employees, he says, are those who thrive on detailed planning and organization. These workers prefer to focus on one task at a time and they follow a schedule from which they don't like to deviate. According to Lindquist, monochrons are rattled by interruptions and tend to put new tasks off until a later date, when they can be worked into the schedule.

Conversely, a polychron prefers to have

many projects underway simultaneously, enjoys changing from activity to activity, and is unruffled by interruptions. Polychronic time managers, Lindquist's research shows, shift goals throughout the day and tend to feel that they have accomplished those goals when it's time to head for home. And unlike their monochronic counterparts, polychrons believe they perform well under pressure.

"We're at the leading edge in the areas of time personality and time style," Lindquist says. "There's not yet universal agreement on these principles, but we're working to establish guidelines and benchmarks so that when you know someone's time personality, you can predict their behavior, and vice versa."

Even at this early stage, however, managers will benefit from identifying their employees' time styles, according to Lindquist. Whereas in the past a struggling worker may have been criticized as inflexible or unorganized, a supervisor exposed to this theory might instead recognize that the person's time management style conflicts with the work required, and shift that employee to another spot within the organization.

Take an accountant or an engineer, for example. The work required is precise, methodical, and detailed—ideal for a monochron. However, put those same employees who excel in their positions into a sales job, where they move from one customer to another, constantly switching gears and responding to the unexpected, and they'll undoubtedly flounder.

"Conflicting time styles are a great source of turmoil in organizations, but managers aren't always able to identify just what the problem is," says Lindquist. "Imagine you're polychronic and working on a team with two monochrons. You're all frustrated with one another, until we explain to you how monochrons and polychrons operate, and suddenly you understand what it will take to work together. Even though we don't fully understand it yet, if we can awaken people to the general issue, that's useful."

Already, the corporate world is responding. Earlier this year, Lindquist presented his work to local business leaders as part of the Haworth College of Business Dean's Breakfast Speakers Series and at the Kalamazoo rotary club. Impressed by the favorable reaction from the Southwest Michigan crowd, Rotary officials recently approached him about addressing the topic at a national meeting in November.

At the least, this new understanding could help managers identify which type of time management training to which they should send their employees, Lindquist says. "You can't send everyone to a monochronic training—these seminars are of little or no use to polychrons. The people who are teaching this time diary stuff should be teaching how monchrons and polychrons should each use the system. Now that really might revolutionize the way we work."

Source. From *Western Michigan University News.*

After your read, there are two steps left in the SQ3R process: **recite** and **review.**

4. Recite

To **recite** is to say something out loud. When you recite after a reading, you try to remember the main ideas of what you read and state the ideas in your own words as much as possible. It's useful to try to talk out loud, but writing about the text in your own words (without looking back at the reading!) can also be a way to recite.

PRACTICE

Without looking back at the article, try to explain the main ideas. Tell a partner what you remember. Or, if you are alone, try talking out loud and pretend that you are telling a friend about what you read. Sometimes it helps to imagine that you are explaining the reading to someone who is a little younger than yourself. This can help you to simplify complicated ideas and language and to focus only on the main ideas.

5. Review

When you review, you look back at any notes or questions you wrote. You might also reread parts of the article that were difficult to recite from memory or that had a lot of new vocabulary words. It's usually best to review a reading at least several hours after you read it, to see how much information you remember.

PRACTICE

Review the article, following the guidelines presented. If you still do not understand some part of the reading, write your question(s) here:_____

_____

_____

▼ *Reading Review and Discussion*

A. Understanding the Reading

1. What is Dr. Lindquist researching?

2. What is "time personality"?

3. What are three examples of "time styles"?

4. Read the statements below that describe how people manage their time. Write a P by the statements that best describe a **polychron.** Write an M by the statements that best describe a **monochron.**

   a. *I like to do one thing at a time.* _____

   b. *I can focus easily on an activity.* _____

   c. *I am comfortable doing several things at the same time.* _____

   d. *I am easily interrupted.* _____

   e. *I like to plan and organize details.* _____

   f. *I like to follow a precise schedule.* _____

   g. *I am not easily interrupted or distracted from a task.* _____

   h. *I work well under pressure.* _____

   i. *I like open-ended, flexible tasks.* _____

   j. *I like to change my activities often.* _____

   k. *I tend to put off new tasks until I can schedule them later.* _____

   l. *I don't perform well under pressure.* _____

   m. *I like precise, detailed work.* _____

5. How might Dr. Lindquist's results be used in the business world or in a workplace?

6. Why is Dr. Lindquist researching this topic? What does he think is the problem with time styles in workplaces?

7. What is Dr. Lindquist a professor of?

B. Applying the Reading

1. Read the list of jobs below. Write a P by the jobs that might be good for a **polychron**. Write an M by the jobs that might be good for a **monochron**. Explain your reasons. Can you think of other jobs for polychrons or monochrons? Are some jobs good for a "balanced" time style?

   artist _____   *construction worker* _____   *lab technician* _____

   musician _____   *accountant* _____   *engineer* _____

   medical doctor _____   *salesperson* _____

2. How does Dr. Lindquist think that understanding different time styles will change the workplace? Do you agree with him? Why or why not?

3. How might Dr. Lindquist's research be used in schools?

C. Connecting to the Reading

1. What is your time management style? Circle the statements in Section A, number 4, that best describe how you manage your time. Are you a polychron? A monochron? Balanced? Compare your time style with a partner.

2. Have you ever experienced a time style conflict? Tell the class or a small group what happened, or write about what happened. How might an understanding of monochronic and polychronic time styles have helped to resolve this conflict? (Hint: If you can't think of a personal experience, try to give an example about other people you know, or imagine a situation in which a time style conflict might happen).

■ Listening Strategies

◎ *Strategy 1A: Note-Taking Basics*

Taking good notes during your lectures is an important part of learning. You will listen more actively, remember more of the class, make connections to your assigned readings, and have a written record of the class content that you can review later for quizzes or tests. Even if the professor gives you a handout or an outline, you should always take notes yourself.

There are many ways to take notes. In this text, you will practice different note-taking strategies and find the system that works best for you. Also, careful listening and good note-taking take practice. Save your notes. With time, you will see improvement. For extra practice, try to apply the listening strategies in this book to lectures that you might hear in other classes, to radio shows, and to the television (the news and documentary shows on public television are two good places to practice note-taking).

Here is a page that shows you a good basic format for note-taking:

	Write the Class Name, Lecture Topic, and Date at the Top of the Page
	• Leave more space on the left margin. When you review your notes, add questions or key words there to help you organize and remember the information.
	• Don't use a complex outline form. Use bullet points, like this list.
	• Write short phrases or key words, not complete sentences.
	• Leave extra space between your points so you can add information later if you need to.
	• Take notes only on one side of the page. When you review your notes later, add information and questions on the other side.
	• If you miss information—a word or a fact—don't stop writing. Leave a space or draw a line _____ and try to get the information from a classmate later, or ask the professor after class.

PRACTICE

Imagine that you are about to listen to part of a lecture from an anthropology class. Prepare a page in your notebook for note-taking. At the top, write the class name (Anthropology), the date, and the topic (Cultural Perceptions of Time). Take a moment to imagine what your notes will look like.

√ **Study Tip: Sit near the Front of the Room**

Sit near the *front* of the room when you attend a lecture—don't hide in the back. You will see and hear much better in the front, and the professor is more likely to notice that you are there and taking notes.

◉ *Strategy 1B: Deciding What to Write Down*

Don't try to write every word the professor says. You can't! Try to take as many notes as you can, using *phrases* or *words*, in a list form. Listen for these things in particular:

- **Names and dates.** Sometimes a professor will write these on the blackboard as well. Anything that is written on a blackboard should go into your notes.
- **Important words/terms and their definitions.** Sometimes these are so important that a professor will repeat them. Repeated information should be written down.
- **Lists of things** (points, reasons, examples, categories). Always listen for words like *first, second, next, in addition* to signal listed items. Chapter 4 will show you more signal words that you can listen for.
- **Main ideas.** Chapter 2 will discuss more specifically how to do this, but for now, listen for statements that mention facts and key words.

- **Repeated information.** If a professor repeats something, it usually for emphasis. Write it down.

PRACTICE

Listen to part of a lecture from an anthropology class called Cross-Cultural Perceptions of Time (Lecture 1). You can listen to the lecture on the audio companion, or your instructor will deliver the lecture using the transcript in Appendix C of this book. Take notes on the paper you prepared.

▼ *Lecture Review and Discussion*

1. Compare your notes with a partner or a small group. What information did you write down? Did you miss any information? Help each other to fill in any blanks.

2. Review: After looking at your notes, put them away and try to explain the information you learned from the lecture.

3. Discuss this question with a group or the class: Are you from a monochronic culture or a polychronic culture? How many people in the group or the class think they are from monochronic cultures? How many think they are from polychronic cultures? What are these cultures?

4. Have you ever experienced a cross-cultural conflict or misunderstanding because of time? Tell a group or the class what happened, or write about it in a journal.

■ Writing Strategies

◎ *Strategy 1A: Brainstorming*

Many people have trouble getting started on writing assignments. Worrying about what to write can lead to procrastination. The longer you wait to get started, the harder it can be to write! A good way to start writing is to use a prewriting strategy called **brainstorming.**

When you brainstorm, think about the topic and write down anything that comes into your mind—a "storm of ideas" from your brain. Write as quickly as you can. Do not erase anything. Write words or phrases, not complete sentences. Do not worry about grammar or spelling. The purpose is to get ideas on the paper so that you can see them.

PRACTICE

For each of these general topics, brainstorm ideas related to them. For each topic, list as many ideas as you can in three to five minutes.

Free Time   *Time Wasters*   *Technology and Time*

◎ *Strategy 1B: Choosing and Prioritizing Ideas*

You probably don't want to include all the ideas from your brainstorming in your final writing assignment. Some ideas might be closely related. Some ideas might not connect to the topic as well as you thought they did. The writing assignment might not be long enough for you to include all of your ideas.

Your next step is to choose the best ideas for the topic. Circle the ideas that you think would be most interesting or most important to include. Try to find at least three ideas from your brainstorming. For a paragraph assignment, find three ideas that could support a topic. For an essay assignment, find three ideas that you could support with more specific examples. Each idea with examples could then become a separate paragraph. (*Note:* For an essay, you may need to do more brainstorming to find examples for the ideas.)

Next, decide on the best order in which to present the ideas. It is usually a good idea to start with the least important idea and end with the most important. This order will give the reader the feeling that your paragraph or essay is "going somewhere"—that it is moving toward your most important point. Also, remember that the last idea will probably stay in the reader's mind.

PRACTICE

Look back at your brainstorming above. Circle the three most interesting or most important ideas. Then write a 3 next to the least important idea, a 2 next to a more important idea, and a 1 next to the most important idea.

● *Writing Task: What Is Your Time Management Style?*

Write about one of the topics below. Your instructor may tell you to write either a paragraph or an essay. You may be able to use the ideas you just practiced for Writing Strategies 1 and 2. You may also do more brainstorming if you like. (For additional information on writing paragraphs and essays, see Chapter 7, pages 201–19.)

1. Write a paragraph or an essay that describes some activities you do in your free time. You may also consider these questions: How much time do these activities require? Do you have enough time to do these activities? How do you find the time to do them?

2. Write a paragraph or an essay that describes some things you do that waste time. You may also consider these questions: What activity makes you feel like you are wasting time? How much time do these activities take away from things that you need to be doing? What can you do to avoid these time wasters?

3. Do you think that technology gives us more free time or less free time? Does it make our schedules easier or more complicated? Explain your opinion in a paragraph or an essay. Use specific examples of technology and your own experience or observations to support your opinion.

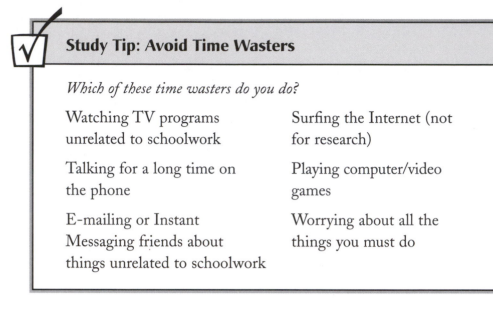

Study Tip: Avoid Time Wasters

Which of these time wasters do you do?

Watching TV programs
unrelated to schoolwork

Surfing the Internet (not
for research)

Talking for a long time on
the phone

Playing computer/video
games

E-mailing or Instant
Messaging friends about
things unrelated to schoolwork

Worrying about all the
things you must do

■ Graphics Strategy

◎ *Strategy 1: Creating a Schedule*

How many hours do you think you spend each week on the following activities?

Attending classes	_____	Sleeping	_____
Commuting to work or to school	_____	Spending time with friends/family	_____
Exercising	_____	Studying	_____
Preparing/eating meals	_____	Working at a job	_____
Running errands	_____	Other? _____	_____

Now see if your guesses are correct! Keep a schedule of your time each day for one week, or write what you did each day in the last week, guessing as closely as possible. Write your activities in the weekly schedule on page 25. Abbreviate if you need to. (See Appendix B for an additional blank schedule.)

	Monday	Tuesday	Wednesday	Thursday	Friday	Saturday	Sunday
7:00–8:00							
8:00–9:00							
9:00–10:00							
10:00–11:00							
11:00–12:00							
12:00–1:00							
1:00–2:00							
2:00–3:00							
3:00–4:00							
4:00–5:00							
5:00–6:00							
6:00–7:00							
7:00–8:00							
8:00–9:00							
10:00–11:00							
11:00–12:00							

DISCUSSION AND PRACTICE

1. Tell the class or a small group about your schedule. Do you have enough time to do everything you want to do? What do you wish you had more time to do? Where do you think you could save time? Are you wasting any time?

2. Compare your chart with a partner's. Give each other advice about how to manage your time.

3. Make a new chart similar to the one on page 25, and write an ideal weekly schedule that will help you to schedule your time more effectively. Tell the class or a small group what changes you made.

✓ Study Tip: The Best Times to Study

Many people study late at night, but most of us are more effective in the morning. Harder tasks are easier to do after a night of sleep. Good times to review readings and notes are immediately after lectures and just before class discussions. You can do shorter study tasks when you are between classes, standing in lines, or waiting for a bus. Finally, if you have five to twenty minutes, you can review notes, formulas, or vocabulary words. Write down things to memorize on 3″ × 5″ index cards and carry them in your pocket.

■ Test-Taking Strategy

◎ *Strategy 1: Planning Your Time, Pacing Yourself*

It's important to manage your time well in a test so that you can complete it all before the time runs out. Sometimes students get "stuck" on a hard question, or spend too much time in one section. Follow these steps for managing your time on a quiz or test.

1. Preview the test.

   • How many questions do you have to answer? How many points are given for each item or section on the test? Usually not all questions are worth the same amount. Spend more time on questions that give you more points. For example, look at the practice test on pages 28–30. Although they look long, Sections A and B are only worth 10 points each. It might be better to spend more time on Section C, which is worth 30 points—each of the three questions is worth more than one point.

   • Read the directions carefully before you start answering questions. Sometimes people waste time because they read the directions incorrectly and they have to go back and change answers—if they still have time. Circle important words that will help you to answer the questions. For example, look at the practice test on pages 28–30. Notice the word *not* in Question 1 of Section A. If you did not read the directions carefully, you might answer the question incorrectly. In Section B, it is important to note that the letter of each definition should be written next to its corresponding word; the items should not be matched by drawing lines to connect the items. If you did not read the directions carefully, you might not receive credit for that part of the test— or you might waste time erasing lines and writing the letters in at the last minute.

2. Pace yourself.

   • Answer the easiest questions first to reduce anxiety: You already know you can answer some questions easily and you'll get points for them. When you're relaxed, you'll be able to focus on the difficult questions.

   • Skip questions you're not sure of. Mark the questions you skip by lightly circling the number. When you go back to the hard questions, try to eliminate wrong answers. You can skip questions throughout the test (for example, skip Section B if you're not sure about definitions, and complete

Sections A and C first). You can also skip items within a section. For example, in Section B of the practice test, you could match the items you are sure about first, then go back and try to match the ones you are not sure about.

- Try to picture where you learned the information for each test item: Was it from a lecture or a reading? Try to visualize (imagine) the page from the textbook or the page from your notes.

PRACTICE

A short test on some of the information presented in this chapter follows. Preview the test, and then use the other strategies presented to answer the questions in 15 or 20 minutes. Pace yourself.

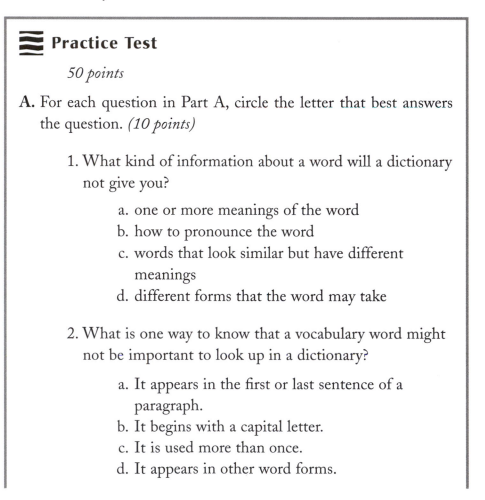

≋ **Practice Test**

50 points

A. For each question in Part A, circle the letter that best answers the question. *(10 points)*

1. What kind of information about a word will a dictionary not give you?
   a. one or more meanings of the word
   b. how to pronounce the word
   c. words that look similar but have different meanings
   d. different forms that the word may take

2. What is one way to know that a vocabulary word might not be important to look up in a dictionary?
   a. It appears in the first or last sentence of a paragraph.
   b. It begins with a capital letter.
   c. It is used more than once.
   d. It appears in other word forms.

3. What kind of information is probably not very important to write down for lecture notes?

    a. main ideas

    b. key words and definitions

    c. names and dates

    d. signal words like *first, second, next, according to, finally*

B. Match each word on the left with its meaning on the right. Write the letter of each definition on the line next to the word. *(10 points)*

1. SQ3R _____

    a. organizing your time and schedule

2. brainstorming _____

    b. activities that distract you from work

3. time management _____

    c. a verb, noun, adjective, or adverb

4. class participation _____

    d. a list of words and information on them

5. time wasters _____

    e. a five-step reading strategy

6. skimming _____

    f. talking in class and group discussions

7. scanning _____

    g. looking over a text to find key features

8. word form _____

    h. delaying work or a task until later

9. vocabulary log _____

    i. reading a text very quickly

10. procrastination _____

    j. quickly writing down ideas about a topic

C. Write a short answer to each of the following questions. *(30 points)*

    1. What are some ways to speak more in class? List at least four:

    _____

    _____

    _____

    _____

    2. What are some ways to preview a reading? List at least three:

    _____

    _____

    _____

    _____

    3. What are some points to remember when taking notes in a basic format? List at least three:

    _____

    _____

    _____

    _____

Orientation

Finding Out about Academic Year Schedules

Colleges usually post a schedule of their academic year on their website or in a *catalogue* or *bulletin* (a book that lists the college's policies, requirements, and courses). The academic schedule tells you when the semester (or quarter) begins and ends and what holidays you will have off. It may also include important deadlines, such as the last day you can add or drop a class. Knowing the academic schedule in advance can help you to plan your own monthly and weekly schedules even before you sign up for classes. You can write down major events in advance. After your classes start, you can create a weekly schedule, writing down the due dates of major assignments, other important commitments (such as work or family responsibilities), and blocks of time for studying.

YOUR TASK

1. If you are currently in a college, find the academic schedule online or in a course bulletin. If you are not currently in a college, use the Internet to find the schedule for a college near you or a college that interests you.

2. Compare your results with a group. Discuss or write answers to these questions:

   a. When does the semester or quarter begin?
   b. When does the semester or quarter end?
   c. Which holidays does the college have off?
   d. What other information did you find on the academic year schedule?

Study Tip: Schedule Downtime

"Downtime" is time that is just for relaxing. It might be watching TV or going to a movie, talking to a friend on the phone, exercising, reading a book for fun, going for a walk, or just doing nothing at all. It's important to have at least a few minutes of downtime for yourself each day. You will feel refreshed and be more focused if you take breaks. Also, don't forget to eat and to sleep! These are priorities too!

▼ *Final Project*

Designing a Time Management Survey

Working with a group, write survey questions to find out how other people in your class or other people you know spend their time. You can use the questions from the Graphics activity on page 24, or write additional questions of your own. Present your findings to the class in a group presentation, or write your results in a short report. Try to use vocabulary and ideas that you learned in this chapter.

In your oral or written report, you might also consider these questions:

- What information was most surprising?
- Which activities seem to be the biggest waste of time?
- Do your results suggest that people work too much or too little?
- Do your results suggest that most people manage their time effectively or ineffectively?

Study Tip: Keep Up with a Course Schedule or Syllabus

On the first day of class, a professor will usually give out a **syllabus** (an explanation of course goals, major assignments, and policies) and a **course schedule** (a week-by-week or day-by-day list of class topics, readings, and homework assignments). Some professors may even post this information on a website. College professors rarely write homework assignments on the blackboard. It is your responsibility to follow the schedule. Usually, readings and assignments listed next to a date must be completed by the beginning of class on that day. If you have difficulty understanding a course schedule, ask the professor to explain it to you.

▼ *Check Your Progress*

How are you doing so far? Put a check mark in the box that best explains how you feel about your progress in each category. Be sure to ask your instructor or classmates for help if there is something that you don't understand or that you would like to review.

Topic	I understand this topic very well; I feel confident about using it again.	I understand most of this topic; I feel moderately confident using it again.	I understand some but not all of this topic.	I don't understand this topic well; I need to review.
Key Words: Using a Dictionary				
Vocabulary Strategy 1A: Deciding Which Words Are Important to Know				
Vocabulary Strategy 1B: Keeping a Vocabulary Log				
Speaking Strategy 1: Understanding "Class Participation" (Ten Tips . . .)				
Reading Strategy 1: SQ3R				
Listening Strategy 1A: Note-Taking Basics				
Listening Strategy 1B: Deciding What to Write Down				
Writing Strategy 1A: Brainstorming				
Writing Strategy 1B: Choosing and Prioritizing Ideas				
Graphics Strategy 1: Creating a Schedule				
Test-Taking Strategy 1: Planning Your Time, Pacing Yourself				
Orientation: Finding Out about Academic Year Schedules				

Which class participation tip(s) did you use?

_____

_____

What was the most important thing you learned in this chapter?

_____

_____

If you checked "do not understand" for anything in the chart on page 33, write a question about that topic:

_____

_____

Look back at the personal learning goals you set in Getting Started on page xxvi. What did you do in this chapter to help yourself meet those goals?

_____

_____

2 ᰔ **Learning**

Warm-Up: What Is Your Learning Style?

Your **learning style** is the way you learn new information. Not everyone has the same learning style. There are many learning styles, but we will focus on three: **visual** (seeing), **auditory** (hearing), and **kinesthetic** (physical/body).

1. Read the words in the column on the left on page 36. Then read across the chart. Circle the statements that best describe how you feel about that word. It's okay to circle more than one statement in a row. Count the number of statements you circled and write the total at the bottom of each column.

	Column 1	Column 2	Column 3
Concentrating	I get distracted by movements or untidy workspaces. I sometimes notice things that other people don't see.	I get distracted by sounds and noises.	I get distracted by activities and conversations around me.
Visualizing	I see clear, detailed pictures in my thoughts.	I think in sounds and voices.	I see images in my thoughts that involve movement.
Talking	I don't like to listen for a long time. I often use words like *see, picture,* and *imagine.*	I enjoy listening. Sometimes I'm impatient to talk. I often use words like *say, hear,* and *think.*	I like to use expressive gestures and movements (nonverbal communication). I often use words like *feel, touch,* and *hold.*
Contacting People	I prefer face-to-face, personal meetings.	I prefer the telephone.	I prefer to talk while walking or doing an activity.
Meeting Someone Again	I forget names but remember faces. I can usually remember where I met someone.	I remember people's names. I can usually remember what we talked about.	I usually remember what we did together, or what it felt like to be with the person.
Relaxing	I prefer to watch TV, see a play, or go to a movie.	I prefer to listen to the radio, play music, read, or talk with a friend.	I prefer to play sports or make something with my hands.
Reading	I like descriptive scenes. Sometimes I stop reading and imagine the action.	I like dialogue. I can "hear" the characters talk.	I like action stories. (OR: I don't really enjoy reading for pleasure.)
Spelling	I try to see the word in my mind. I imagine what it looks like on paper.	I try to sound out the word. I hear it in my thoughts or say it out loud.	I write down the word to find out if it "feels" right. I might type the word or even touch the word on the page.
Learning something new	I like to see demonstrations, diagrams, pictures, and charts.	I like verbal and written instructions. I like talking about the subject with people.	I prefer to learn something by doing it right away. I keep trying, and I might try something in different ways.
Putting something together	I look at the picture first; after that, I might read the directions.	I like reading or talking with someone about it. Sometimes I talk out loud as I work.	I usually don't look at directions. I figure it out as I go along.
Understanding how people feel	I mostly look at facial expressions.	I listen to the sound or tone of their voice.	I look at their body language.
Teaching people	I prefer to show people things.	I prefer to tell people things or write them out.	I prefer to demonstrate how something is done and ask them to try it.
TOTAL	Visual_____	Auditory_____	Kinesthetic_____

Source: Adapted from *Learn More Now: 10 Steps to Learning Better, Smarter, and Faster.*

If you circled mostly statements in Column 1, you are a visual learner.

If you circled mostly statements in Column 2, you are an auditory learner.

If you circled mostly statements in Column 3, you are a kinesthetic learner.

Some people have a combination of learning styles. Do you?

Write your learning style(s) here: _____

2. Take a class survey. Find out how many people in your class are visual, auditory, and kinesthetic learners.

3. Now ask your instructor to take this same test. What kind of learner is your instructor? Does his or her learning style match the learning style of most of the people in the class?

4. Brainstorm in small groups or as a class: What are some ways that visual learners might learn well? Auditory learners? Kinesthetic learners? Compare your brainstorming results with the study tips for different learning styles that you will find throughout this chapter.

Key Words

Read the words in the box. You will see these key words used in this chapter. Circle the words you don't know. Use a dictionary to check the meanings. Then match the words to their definitions. Pay attention to word form.

adjust	enable	linguistic	perception	spatial
auditory	kinesthetic	logical	recall	theory

1. enable	_____	a. remember information or events
2. recall	_____	b. an idea that has not been proven
3. spatial	_____	c. related to space/distance
4. theory	_____	d. uses reasoning and proof
5. auditory	_____	e. help
6. perception	_____	f. related to movement
7. adjust	_____	g. related to hearing
8. linguistic	_____	h. change, modify
9. kinesthetic	_____	i. understanding of something
10. logical	_____	j. related to language

■ Vocabulary Strategy

◉ Strategy 2: Looking for Definition Signals near a Word

Sometimes you can guess the meaning of a word without using a dictionary by looking for definition signals that might appear near the word. Here are some questions to ask when looking for definitions near a word.

- Is there a **definition phrase near the word?** Look for key words that often introduce definitions: *in other words, this means that, refers to, which is, known as, or.* (For example: Metacognition, or thinking about thinking, is an important part of the classroom experience. *Or thinking about thinking* is a definition.)
- Is there **unusual punctuation after the word?** Sometimes definitions follow a dash (—) or a colon (:). Definitions can also appear in parentheses following a word (like this).
- Are there **examples of the word?** Look for key words that introduce examples: *such as, for example, an example of this is, to illustrate, like.*
- Are there **synonyms** (words with the same or a similar meaning)? For example, *smart* and *bright* have similar meanings.
- Are there **antonyms** (words with the opposite or a contrasting meaning)?

- Are there **short explanations in the margins or in footnotes at the bottom of the page?** Look outside the paragraph or passage. Textbooks often define key words in other places for quick reference.

PRACTICE

Read this passage from an Introduction to a psychology textbook. Look for definition signals near the highlighted or shaded words. Then complete the chart that follows.

RECALLING LONG-TERM MEMORIES

Have you ever tried to remember someone's name, convinced that you knew it, but unable to recall it no matter how hard you tried? This not infrequent occurrence—known as the tip-of-the-tongue phenomenon—exemplifies the difficulties that can occur in retrieving information stored in long-term memory.

tip-of-the-tongue phenomenon: the inability to recall information that one realizes one knows—a result of the difficulty of retrieving information from long-term memory

Retrieval Cues

One reason recall is not perfect is the sheer quantity of recollections that are stored in long-term memory. Although the issue is far from settled, many psychologists have suggested that the material that makes its way there is relatively permanent. If they are correct, this suggests that the capacity of long-term memory is vast, given the broad range of people's experiences and educational backgrounds. For instance, if you are like the average college student, your vocabulary includes some 50,000 words, you know hundreds of mathematical "facts," and you are able to conjure up images—such as the way your childhood home looked—with no trouble at all. In fact, simply cataloging all your memories would probably take years of work.

How do we sort through this vast array of material and retrieve specific information at the appropriate time? One of the major ways is through the use of retrieval cues. A *retrieval cue* is a stimulus that allows us to recall information that is located in long-term memory more easily. It may be a word, an emotion, a sound; whatever the specific cue, a memory will suddenly come to mind when the retrieval cue is present. For example, the smell of roasting turkey may evoke memories of Thanksgiving or family gatherings.

Source: From *Essentials of Understanding Psychology, 3rd ed.*

Now complete the word chart.

Word	Possible Meaning	Type of Definition Signal
1. tip-of-the-tongue phenomenon		
2. recollections		
3. vast		
4. images		
5. retrieval cue		

REVIEW

1. Are the highlighted words important to know? Why or why not? What other words in this passage are important to know?

2. Add these words, or five important words of your choice, to your Vocabulary Log. Or you can use words from the reading on pages 44–47.

Study Tip: Use Visual Learning Strategies

Are you a visual learner? Draw pictures in the margins to help you remember what you read. Pay close attention to pictures, charts, and graphs in your readings. Use different colors to mark your readings and notes. Think about the topic like it's a movie—close your eyes and picture what happens.

■ Speaking Strategy

◎ *Strategy 2: Participating in Small Group Discussions*

In some classes or discussion sections, your professor may divide the class into small groups to discuss questions or to do an activity. It's very important to participate as much as you can in a small group. It's one way to show the professor that you are participating in class. Also, it's good practice for your speaking and listening skills.

Sometimes the hardest part of a small group discussion is keeping the discussion going. It's a good idea to choose group members to do the following kinds of jobs:

> **Discussion Leader:** Makes sure that the group stays focused and completes the task. Uses phrases to keep conversation going and to get everyone to participate: *What do you think? Does anyone disagree? Does everyone agree? Does anyone have any other ideas? What's another way to look at this question?*

> **Scribe:** Takes notes on the group discussion. Uses phrases for clarification: *Can you repeat that? Did you mean to say . . . ? Is there anything else you'd like to add?*

> **Reporter:** Reports back to the class after the small-group discussion; tells everyone what the group discussed. May use the secretary's notes. Uses phrases like: *Our group discussed . . . ; we felt that . . . ; we agreed about . . . ; we disagreed about . . . ; Some people said that . . . ; Others said that . . .*

PRACTICE

The next time you work with a small group, choose a job from the list above. Use the phrases for that job in your small group discussions and activities in this chapter.

☑ **Study Tip: Plan Your Reading Time**

Are you an auditory learner? Try reading aloud or "talking to" the text—ask it questions, imagine you are having a conversation with it. Form a study group, or find a study partner and talk about what you read and learned.

■ Reading Strategy

◎ *Strategy 2: Identifying Main Ideas and Supporting Details*

The main ideas of paragraphs are often stated in *topic sentences*. Topic sentences can also state an opinion about the topic. The topic sentence is then supported with specific details and examples. In academic writing, the topic sentence is almost always the first sentence of a paragraph. However, sometimes it can be found in the middle of the paragraph or at the end. Sometimes, especially in newspaper and magazine writing, it is implied—it is not directly stated.

REVIEW

Use SQ3R as you read the article on pages 44–47. Follow the same steps you used on pages 12–16 of Chapter 1. Write your questions in the margins of this reading or in your class notebook.

PRACTICE

When you read the article, find the main ideas / topic sentences of each paragraph. Underline, highlight, or write them on a separate piece of paper.

✓ **Study Tip: Be Aware of Citations as You Read**

Sometimes in a more complex article or textbook chapter, you will come across **citations**. Citations indicate where a writer got other ideas or information. They give basic information like the author's last name and the year in which that person's work was published, along with a page number. A citation may look like this: (Gardner, 1983, p. 173). You may also see a footnote, which is a small number after a sentence or line, like this.[1] The number may refer a reader to the bottom of a page or to pages at the end of the article, where complete information about the source can be found. It can be useful to look at someone else's sources to see what they read, especially if you are writing a research paper. For the readings in this textbook, however, you do not need to worry about the citation information—just recognize that you may see it from time to time.

Multiple Intelligences in the Classroom: Characteristics of the Eight Types of Intelligences as Identified by Howard Gardner

Jennifer L. Nolen

In order to address the need for different teaching strategies, we must first realize there are different learning styles. Howard Gardner was aware of this when he developed his theory of multiple intelligences. According to Gardner, there are eight kinds of intelligences. Howard Gardner's theory of multiple intelligences requires teachers to adjust their instructional strategies in order to meet students' individual needs.

The first of Gardner's intelligences is linguistic or verbal. Verbal intelligence involves the mastery of language. People with verbal intelligence tend to think in words and have highly developed auditory skills. They are frequently reading or writing. Their ability to manipulate language lends them to fields such as teaching, journalism, writing, law, and translation. Language enables them to be better at memorizing information. Verbal students are often great storytellers and joke tellers.

Linguistic intelligence enables one to pay special attention to grammar and vocabulary. They have great ability to use words with clarity. These people can use this to their own benefit either to explain, persuade, or entertain . . . .

In order for teachers to help linguistic learners progress, they need to use language that the student can relate to and fully comprehend. If used correctly, language can provide a bridge between the material and the learner. Having children write, read, and give oral reports about an element in their own lives such as sports, television, or popular bands develops their linguistic intelligence.

Music and language can be considered a common medium. Yet, they have evolved on separate courses. Musical intelligence, therefore, is the next of the multiple intelligences.

Musical intelligence makes use of sound to the greatest extent possible. Those with musical intelligence have a firm understanding of pitch, rhythm, and timbre. Through music, they are able to convey their emotions. Often, this intelligence is discovered at an early age. The individual differences between those with musical intelligence and those without are apparent from the day a child learns to sing. These students are usually able to read music, critique performances, and to use musical-critical categories.

Our culture is known to minimize the importance of music and music education. Teachers should foster musical intelligence by introducing "formal musical analysis and representation" (Gardner, 1983, p. 111). Music can act as a way of capturing feelings, of knowing and understanding feelings, which is an important part of educating children. Another reason musical intelligence should be valued is that it can be tied to other intelligences. For example, it relates to the logical-mathematical intelligence in that music also contains ratio and regularity, as well as mathematical patterns.

Mathematical-logical intelligence consists of the ability to detect patterns, reason deductively, and think logically. Children first explore this intelligence by ordering and re-ordering objects. They begin math using material objects such as marbles or M&Ms. After time passes, children are able to do math in their heads without the use of manipulatives. As this intelligence grows, the love of abstraction separates those with mathematical intelligence from the rest. They are able to follow long chains of reasoning very skillfully. These are usually the children who do well in the traditional classroom because they are able to follow the logical sequencing behind the teaching and are, therefore, able to conform to the role of model student. Another advantage is that they are able to calculate very quickly . . . .

Spatial intelligence gives a person the ability to manipulate and create mental images in order to solve problems. Spatial thinkers "perceive the visual world accurately, to perform transformations and modifications

upon one's initial perceptions, and to be able to re-create aspects of one's initial perceptions, even in the absence of relevant physical stimuli" (Gardner, 1983, p. 173). Spatial intelligence can lend itself to the ability of visual perception, while lacking in the ability to draw, imagine, or transform or vice versa . . . .

Spatial intelligence empowers hunters and travelers—giving them better accuracy and less of a chance of getting lost. A navigator or guide possesses a great deal of this intelligence, as does an architect or lighting designer. People with spatial intelligence often like playing chess, a lot of color, and to imagine the world differently.

The role that spatial intelligence plays in the visual arts is evident. Painting and sculpting often rely on spatial thinking. An artist's style often depends on their ability to visualize and create from a blank canvas.

Children with spatial intelligence are best taught using pictures or photographs. It is often a good assessment to have them draw their ideas. These students also benefit from films, overheads, diagrams, and other such visuals . . . .

Bodily-kinesthetic intelligence entails the ability to understand the world through the body. These people can use their body in very expressive skilled ways for a distinct purpose. They have very fine motor skills of the fingers and hands and control of their gross motor movements. These characteristics go together with their ability to manipulate objects, and to carry out delicate movements using precise control.

These abilities lead people into professions such as surgeons, sculptors, carpenters, plumbers, athletes, dancers, and mimes. Dancers use "patterned sequences of nonverbal body movements that are purposeful, intentionally rhythmic and have aesthetic value in the eyes of those for whom the dancer is performing" (Gardner, 1983, p. 222). Performers are able to capture the intended emotion and express them through different mediums. Kinesthesis is the capacity to act gracefully and to apprehend directly the actions of the dynamic abilities of other people or objects. This is what makes people with bodily intelligence good at the performing arts. Another beneficiary of bodily intelligence is the athlete. Exceptional athletes are graceful, powerful, fast, and accurate, and they can use these abilities to develop precise timing to better their game.

Teaching children with bodily-kinesthetic intelligence can be optimized through the use of manipulatives and physical movement. These children like to touch things in order to learn, they usually cannot sit still for long. They enjoy keeping their hands busy; therefore different learning tools should be brought into the classroom to accommodate these students. These students may seem fidgety during much of the class. Simply giving them something to keep in their hands might solve this problem. Corporations have seen this in their meetings, so they have brought "executive toys" into their meetings. Each member is given some

sort of gizmo to keep his or her hands busy. It has been found to increase creativity and productivity significantly. The same effect could take place with bodily-kinesthetic students, and it may just be that they needed something in their hands to satisfy this urge and calm their brains so that thinking and learning can take place . . . .

The interpersonal intelligence consists of the ability to understand, perceive, and discriminate between people's moods, feelings, motives, and intelligences. Interpersonal intelligence shares many of its characteristics with intrapersonal intelligence. Intrapersonal deals more with the individual self. It is the ability to know oneself and to understand one's own inner workings. These personal intelligences are often seen as the highest achievement made by human beings. They are both information-processing capacities available to every human from infancy.

Those with interpersonal intelligences are often found in professions such as teaching, politics, religious leaders such as Gandhi or Martin Luther King Junior, salesmen, skilled parents, therapists, or counselors. Cult leaders and people like Adolf Hitler have been known to have high degrees of interpersonal intelligence, proving that it can also be used for things other than good.

People with intrapersonal intelligence are usually imaginative, original, patient, disciplined, motivated, and have a great deal of self-respect. This intelligence is developed from internal resources. In everyday class, children with intrapersonal characteristics need to be praised frequently. Much of the development of intrapersonal intelligence depends on how the student wishes to use it. It can be aided through imagination exercises. They could be given long-term projects with various stages that need to be checked before moving on to the next. This will help the students strengthen their abilities of patience and procedure. These students can see what needs to be done in their minds, then will make it happen.

The interpersonal intelligence can be fostered through having students work together. The learning and the use of a culture's symbol system leads to development of interpersonal intelligence. Much of the personal intelligences is basic and does not require much from others. Observation and experience are the most appropriate tools to further these intelligences.

Another intelligence that benefits from observation and experience is environmental or naturalist intelligence. Environmental intelligence is Gardner's latest, but probably not his last, intelligence. It involves the ability to understand nature's symbols, to respect the delicate balance that lets us continue to live. They have a genuine appreciation of the aspects of nature and how they intertwine. They put the future of the world first and are concerned about how man could be destroying or disrupting our planet for future generations. People with naturalistic intelligence often show expertise in the recognition and classification of plants and animals.

Naturalists can be anyone from a molecular biologist to a traditional man who uses herbal remedies. George Washington Carver, Rachel Carson, and Charles Darwin are often considered to have had naturalist intelligence. A child who is exceptionally good at sorting and classifying rocks, insects, shells, or dinosaurs is another example of a naturalist.

These children often benefit from learning outdoors. Teachers can accommodate for them by planning activities such as: observing nature, labeling and mounting specimens from nature, noticing changes in the environment, sorting articles from nature, using binoculars or telescopes to study nature, [taking] nature hikes or field trips in nature, caring for pets, and so forth. These activities allow the student to have a hands on experience with what they are most comfortable doing.

All of the intelligences described throughout this article are a better way for teachers to understand and accommodate different learning styles. Teachers should structure the presentation of material in a style which engages all or most of the intelligences. When teachers center lessons on the students' needs, it optimizes learning for the whole class. Teachers who teach towards the multiple intelligences realize the benefits such as active learners and successful students. Each of the intelligences is potential in every learner, and it is part of a teacher's job to nurture and help the children develop their own intelligences.

Source: From *Education.*

▼ *Reading Review and Discussion*

A. Understanding the Reading

1. What are the eight types of intelligence according to Howard Gardner?

2. According to the author of this article, why should teachers understand these eight intelligences?

3. Complete this chart with information from the reading. If you can't complete the chart from memory, look back at the main ideas you underlined and find the information. The first one is done for you as an example.

Intelligence Type	Description of people with this intelligence	Good jobs for people with this intelligence	Ways that teachers can teach people with this intelligence
linguistic/verbal	Think in words, often read or write, have good listening skills, pay attention to grammar and vocabulary, use words well, can be good storytellers and joke tellers	Teaching, journalism, writing, law, translation	Use language that students can relate to and understand; have students read, write, and give oral reports

B. Applying the Reading

1. Look at the third column of the chart on page 48. Can you think of additional jobs that might be good for each intelligence type? Discuss your ideas with a small group, and write your answers in the chart. Are some jobs good for more than one intelligence type? Which ones? Why?

2. This article is mostly concerned with how Gardner's theory of multiple intelligences applies to children in the classroom. Do you think that this theory is also important for students in college classrooms? Why or why not?

3. Read the last sentence of the article again. Do you agree that it is the teacher's responsibility to nurture (or accommodate) students' different intelligence types? Do you think that teachers should do more to accommodate different learning styles? Or, do you think that students should adjust their learning styles to fit with their teachers' teaching style? Discuss this issue with a small group. Give specific reasons for your opinion. Try to come to an agreement or some kind of conclusion as a group.

C. Connecting to the Reading

1. Look back at your notes in the chart on page 48. Which description best fits you? What is your intelligence type? Do you have more than one intelligence? How does your intelligence type compare with the results of your learning style test at the beginning of the chapter? Which description more accurately describes you? Compare your answer with a partner or group.

2. Think about how you were taught in school when you were younger, or how you are taught in classes now. Do you think that your teachers used strategies that worked with your intelligence type? Why or why not?

> ☑ **Study Tip: Use Kinesthetic Learning Strategies**
>
> Are you a kinesthetic learner? If you are, write a lot in your book—mark or highlight passages that are important to you. Hold the book in your hands when you read; try walking around while you read. Stay active.

■ Listening Strategy

◎ *Strategy 2: Taking Notes in a Block System*

	Write the lecture topic and date at the top of the page
	Write each main topic as a header or a question.
	Listen for signal words and phrases that can introduce
	main topics: *First, Second, Third, Next, Finally, Most/Least*
	Important. Also, your instructor may give you the main
	topics in an outline form at the beginning of the lecture.
	Skip lines between blocks of information or paragraphs.
	Beneath each main topic heading, indent and write down
	as many details as you can in paragraph or block form. You
	don't have to use complete sentences like you would in a
	regular paragraph. Phrases are fine. So are key words.

PRACTICE

Prepare your paper for note-taking. Listen to part of a lecture from a psychology class (Lecture 2) called Three Systems of Memory. You can listen to the lecture on the audiotape, or your instructor will deliver the lecture using the transcript in Appendix C of this book. Listen for main ideas and details. Take notes using the block method.

▼ *Lecture Review and Discussion*

Divide into three groups according to the three main learning styles: visual, auditory, and kinesthetic. Sit with other people who have a similar primary learning style as yours.

1. **Compare your lecture notes.** What information did you write down? Did you miss any information? Help each other to fill in any blanks.

2. **Review.** With your group, go over your notes and apply one of the study tips for your learning style. If you are visual learners, draw pictures or diagrams to illustrate the information you learned. If you are auditory learners, talk about what you remember and learned from the lecture. If you are kinesthetic learners, prepare a short skit or a physical presentation, using your bodies, to demonstrate the material that you learned from the lecture.

3. **Share your group's note review strategy with the class.** Discuss the differences in learning styles that you noticed.

■ Writing Strategy

◎ *Strategy 2: Clustering*

Clustering, like brainstorming, helps you to put ideas onto paper and decide what you will include in a writing assignment. When you brainstorm, you list ideas quickly. When you cluster, you group related ideas and look for connections between ideas.

First, in the center of a page, write a word, phrase, or expression related to the topic of your writing assignment. Draw a circle around it. Next, write down any other words, phrases, or expressions that come to mind when you think of your topic. These could also include facts, examples, details, quotations, and questions. Circle these new words and draw lines to the center word. Draw lines between new words and ideas that seem to connect. Keep adding new words and ideas, circling them, and connecting them to related ideas. Each group of related ideas is a "cluster." Sometimes a cluster contains the "seeds" of a paragraph; several clusters might be the "seeds" of an essay.

Here is an example of a clustering activity for a writing assignment about education.

PRACTICE

Draw a cluster map for each of these topics for a writing assignment:

My Learning Style   *Learning Styles in My Class*   *Teaching Styles*

● *Writing Task: Learning/Teaching Styles*

Write about one of the topics below. Your instructor will let you know whether to write a paragraph or an essay. Use ideas from your cluster map. You may add more ideas to your cluster map if you like. Refer to Chapter 7 for more information about writing paragraphs and essays.

1. Write a paragraph or an essay that describes your learning style or styles. Use specific examples from your experience to explain your learning style(s).

2. Write a paragraph or an essay that describes the dominant learning style or styles in your class. Use specific examples from your observations or from your discussions with classmates.

3. Do you think that teachers should do more to work with different learning styles? Explain your opinion in a paragraph or an essay. To support your opinion, use specific examples from your experience, observations, discussions, or the reading in this chapter.

■ Graphics Strategy

◎ *Strategy 2: Creating a Hierarchical Map*

When you review lecture notes or a textbook, writing your notes in a graphic form will help you to visualize the relationship between ideas. A *hierarchy* is a system that ranks things from most important (on the top) to the least important (on the bottom). A **hierarchical map** shows the relationship of the main ideas to the supporting details, starting with the main ideas. Here is an example of a hierarchical map to illustrate part of the lecture you just listened to.

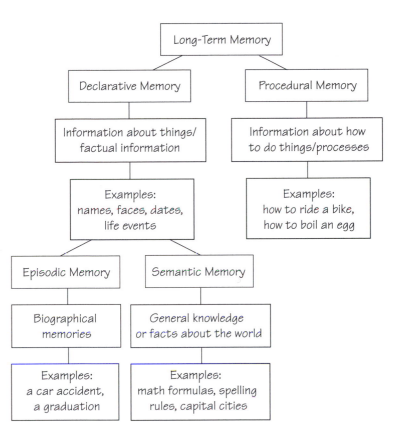

PRACTICE

Review the Chapter Reading on pages 44–47. Write notes in the form of a hierarchical map.

■ Test-Taking Strategy

◎ *Strategy 2: Interpreting Multiple-Choice Questions*

Multiple-choice tests are the most common type of test. Multiple-choice questions have two parts: a *stem* (a question or an unfinished statement) and *possible answers*. Here are some strategies for taking tests with this type of question.

- Read the question and all of the possible answers, even if you think you see the "correct" answer right away. Sometimes there are better choices.
- Read the question, cover the possible answers, and try to think of the answer on your own. Then compare your answer to the possible answers.
- Look for answer choices that you know are wrong. Keep eliminating incorrect answers until only one remains. This answer is probably the correct one.
- Identify **distractors**. Wrong answer choices are meant to distract you from the correct answer. Distractors may contain very general language. A correct answer is more likely to use specific language or detailed information. Distractors may also contain unfamiliar terms (made-up terms or terms from other material).
- Watch out for answer choices that are opposites. One of them is probably the correct answer.
- Look for words in the answer choices that are similar to words used in the stem: Synonyms, as well as different word forms of the same word, can be clues that an answer choice may be correct. On the other hand, these can also be distractors designed to confuse you. Sometimes an instructor will use a word in an answer choice that looks similar to a word in the stem but in fact has a very different meaning.

Here is a sample test item and an example of how someone might work through it.

Which of the following activities would best describe an auditory learner?

    a. likes to watch TV and remembers faces well

    b. likes to listen to music and talk with other people

    c. likes to audition for theatre productions

    d. likes to talk while walking or doing an activity

Hopefully, you would remember the description of an auditory learner that was given earlier in this chapter. If not, hopefully you remembered that *auditory* has to do with hearing. Therefore, option **c** can be eliminated. *Audition* looks similar to *auditory* but does not have the same meaning; to audition is to try to get a part in a play or some other kind of production. It does not really describe a learning style. Option **d** can be eliminated too; although talking has something to do with hearing, the emphasis in that statement is on walking and doing an activity—both physical activities describing a different learning style. Option **a** can be eliminated because it contains visual details—watching, remembering faces—that don't relate to hearing. This leaves the correct answer, **b,** remaining. Since the word *listen* is a synonym for *hear,* and both music and talk relate to hearing, you can feel confident that **b** is the correct answer.

Here is another example:

> Which of the following activities would best describe a visual learner?
>
> a. uses words like *feel, touch,* and *hold*
>
> b. likes to advise others
>
> c. does not usually look at directions or maps when learning something new or going somewhere unfamiliar
>
> d. learns well from seeing pictures, diagrams, and charts

Hopefully, you would remember the description of a visual learner that was given earlier in this chapter. If not, hopefully you remembered that *visual* has to do with vision or seeing. Therefore, option **a** can be eliminated; the activities of feeling, touching, and holding do not require the ability to see. Option **b** can be eliminated too; although *advise* might look like *visualize* (the letters *vis* are present), the word has nothing to do with vision. Also, option **b** is a little too general compared to the other answer choices. (Likes to advise other about what?) That leaves options **c** and **d.** Notice that both options have synonyms of *visual: look at* and *seeing.* There are also references to specific things that someone can see: *directions, maps, pictures, diagrams,* and *charts.* Therefore, you need to look very closely at **c** and **d.** Notice the negative words in option **c:** *does NOT usually look at.* Options **c** and **d** give opposite ideas. Therefore, **c** can be eliminated, and you are left with **d** as the correct answer: an affirmative statement that uses specific language to describe a quality of a visual learner.

PRACTICE

Use the strategies discussed to work through the following multiple choice test items. Be aware of which strategies you are using to answer each item.

1. Which of the following is not a definition signal?

    a. a definition that you look up in a dictionary

    b. punctuation immediately following the word such as long dashes (—) or colons (:)

    c. phrases like *in other words* . . .

    d. short explanations in the margin or at the bottom of a page

2. Which statement best describes *clustering?*

    a. cleaning clutter off of a desk

    b. writing down ideas and putting related ideas into groups

    c. writing very quickly

    d. getting ideas for a writing assignment

3. What is a hierarchical map?

    a. a drawing and directions showing how to go somewhere efficiently

    b. a graphic representation that helps you to visualize something

    c. a diagram that shows how main ideas and supporting ideas (or most important to least important ideas) relate

    d. a chart that organizes people from the most important to the least important

Study Tip: Use Rehearsal Strategies to Improve Memory

Use *rehearsal strategies* to improve memory. Repeating information from a list, underlining and highlighting, copying, reciting information, and rereading help to move information from short-term to long-term memory.

Orientation

Finding Out about Campus Learning Centers

Most colleges have a learning center (also sometimes called an Academic Resource Center or an Educational Resource Center). This is a place where you can get extra help from tutors in certain subject areas, including math and writing. The tutors are usually college students who have very good grades in these subjects. Some learning centers have graduate students or professional specialists who can help people with reading or ESL. Some offer study groups and special workshops.

YOUR TASK

1. If you are currently in or near a college, find out if the college has a learning center. If it does not, find out what other resources it has for extra help. If you are not currently in or near a college, use the Internet to research a college that interests you online and find out if it has a learning center. Learning centers usually have their own website. Find the following kinds of information:

   Where is the Learning Center? _____

   When is the Learning Center open? _____

   Who works in the Learning Center? _____

   In what subjects can you get help? _____

   What other resources can you find in the Learning Center?_____

   _____

   How do you get help at the center? Do you need to make an appointment?_____

   _____

2. Compare your results with a small group or share them with the class.

Study Tip: Use Tricks to Memorize Information

Mnemonics (pronounced "ni-mon-iks") are memory tricks to help you retrieve information from your memory. You can make up a rhyme or poem to remember something. Or invent *acronyms*, which are words that are made up of the first letter of other words. For example, you can remember the names of the planets of our solar system by memorizing this sentence: "My Very Earnest Mother Just Served Us Nine Pies." Mercury, Venus, Earth, Mars, Jupiter, Saturn, Uranus, Neptune, Pluto.

▼ Final Project

Designing a Learning Styles Survey

Working with a partner or a group, write survey questions to find out how other people in your class or your school like to learn. You can use the chart from the warm-up activity on page 36 to help you, or write questions of your own. Present your findings to the class in a group presentation, or write your results in a short report. Try to use vocabulary and information that you learned in this chapter.

▼ *Check Your Progress*

How are you doing so far? Put a check mark in the box that best explains how you feel about your progress in each category. Be sure to ask your instructor or classmates for help if there is something that you don't understand or that you would like to review.

Topic	I understand this topic very well; I feel confident about using it again.	I understand most of this topic; I feel moderately confident.	I understand some but not all of this topic.	I don't understand this topic well; I need to review.
Key Words				
Vocabulary Strategy 2: Looking for Definition Signals				
Speaking Strategy 2: Participating in Small Group Discussions				
Reading Strategy 2: Identifying Main Ideas and Supporting Details				
Listening Strategy 2: Taking Notes in a Block System				
Writing Strategy 2: Clustering				
Graphics Strategy 2: Creating a Hierarchical Map				
Test-Taking Strategy 2: Interpreting Multiple-Choice Questions				
Orientation: Finding Out about Campus Learning Centers				

Which class participation tip(s) from Chapter 1 did you use?

_____

_____

Which small group participation job(s) did you do?

_____

_____

What was the most important thing you learned in this chapter?

_____

_____

If you checked "do not understand" for anything in the chart on page 61, write a question about that topic:

_____

_____

Look back at the personal learning goals you set in "Getting Started" on page xxvi. What did you do in this chapter to help yourself meet those goals?

_____

_____

3 ∽ Communities

1. How many kinds of groups do you belong to? Complete the chart below by writing down communities or organizations that you are a part of.

National, Racial, or Ethnic Groups	Linguistic Groups (people who speak a certain language)	Social Organizations and Clubs (athletic, musical, etc.)	Professional/Job Organizations (a workplace, memberships, etc.)	Other groups?

2. Which statement best describes how you would define a community?

   a. A community is based on **place**. It is any group of people who live near each other, go to school together, or work together.

   b. A community is based on **social connections and shared activities**.

   c. A community is based on shared **values, beliefs, and ideas**.

3. Look at the groups you listed in the chart on page 63. Decide if each group is primarily a community based on place, social connections/shared activities, or values. Write a **P** (place), **S** (social connections/shared activities), or **V** (values) by each group.

4. Share your chart in a small group. Does anyone in your group belong to the same communities? Which ones?

5. Discuss with your group: What kinds of conflicts can occur among people in a community? Between different communities? List types of conflicts.

6. With your group, decide on a definition of *community* that you can all agree on. What makes a community? Write your definition, using specific examples of communities that fit your definition, and share it with the class.

Key Words

Read the words in the box. You will see these key words used in this chapter. Circle the words you don't know. Use a dictionary to check the meanings. Then use the words to complete the sentences. Pay attention to word form.

characteristics	ethnicity	generalization	integrate	values
dominant	excluded	identity	interact	voluntary

1. Different cultures may have very different _____. For example, some cultures believe that responsibilities to family and community are the most important, while other cultures place more emphasis on the individual.

2. Lee's _____ is very mixed. She is part Korean, Norwegian, and Native American.

3. What are the _____ of a good student? Some qualities of a good student include study skills, a desire to succeed, and the ability to create a strong support system.

4. There is a student lounge at Shorewood Community College where students can meet and talk informally. It's good to have a place where students can _____ outside of class.

5. Commuter students at our college sometimes felt that they weren't a part of the community because they didn't live on campus. Therefore, they asked the school to create more activities to _____ the commuter students and the residential students, bringing the whole community together.

6. Some students in class are too _____. They talk more than everyone else, so it's hard for others to have a chance to speak.

7. The idea that men are better than women at math is just a _____. I know many women who are very good at math.

8. At first, the ESL student club was only open to international students. However, bilingual students felt _____, so the club decided to include them too. Now the club is open to anyone who speaks another language besides English.

9. Thuy is a college student, but that is only one part of her _____. She is also a part-time dental assistant, an aunt, and an award-winning artist.

10. Community service—working for free to help a community in some way—is usually _____. However, some schools now make community service a graduation requirement.

■ Vocabulary Strategy

◎ Strategy 3: Identifying Suffixes and Word Forms

A good dictionary will tell you the different forms of a word. However, looking up every word and word form in a dictionary takes too much time. By looking at the letters at the end of a word, we can usually tell whether a word is a noun, verb, adjective, or adverb. These word forms often have common patterns of letters at the end, or **suffixes**. Common suffixes for different parts of speech are listed below. Notice that some different word forms can use the same suffix. In the chart, circle the suffixes that can be used with more than one part of speech. When you find words with these endings, you will need to pay more attention to the surrounding words in the sentence to determine the word's function.

Noun Suffixes	Verb Suffixes	Adjective Suffixes	Adverb Suffixes
-ment *-ness* *-tion, -sion* *-ict* *-ist* *-ity* *-ology, -ologist* *-er* *-ence* *-ance* *-sure* *-s, -es* (plural)	*-ed* (past tense) *-ing* (progressive tense) *-ate* *-ize*	*-ed* *-ing* *-ible* *-able* *-ary* *-ise* *-ic* *-y* *-al* *-ful* *-ive* *-inct* *-ive* *-er* (comparative) *-est* (superlative)	*-ly* (Be careful! There are some exceptions. *Friendly* looks like an adverb, but it is really an adjective. Always look at the other words in the sentence. And verbs modify verbs or adjectives, not nouns. Examples: *The students were friendly. / The friendly students started a study group.*)

PRACTICE

1. Underline the suffix of each word in the Key Word box (page 64). Determine the form (or possible forms) of each word.

2. Read the passage on page 67 from a sociology textbook. Underline the suffix of each highlighted word. Determine the form of each word (noun, verb, adjective, or adverb). Then write the words in the chart that follows the reading.

The Role of Groups

In the most general sense, a **group** is two or more persons who do the following:

1. Share a distinct identity (the ability to speak a specific language; the biological children of a specific couple; team members; or soldiers);
2. Feel a sense of belonging; and
3. Interact directly or indirectly with [each other].

Groups vary according to a whole host of characteristics, including size, cohesion, purpose, and duration. Sociologists identify primary groups, in-groups, and outgroups as particularly important groups.

Primary Groups

A **primary group**, such as a family or a high school sports team, is characterized by face-to-face contact and strong ties among its members. Primary groups are not always united by harmony and love; for example, they can be united by hatred for another group. In either case, the ties are emotional. The members of a primary group strive to achieve "some desired place in the thoughts of [the] others" and feel allegiance to the other members (Cooley 1909, p. 24). Although a person may never achieve the desired place, he or she may remain preoccupied with that goal. In this sense, primary groups are "fundamental in forming the social nature and ideals of the individual" (Cooley 1909, p. 23). The family is an important primary group because it gives the individual his or her deepest and earliest experiences with relationships and because it gives newcomers their first exposure to the "rules of life." In addition, the family can serve to buffer its members against the effects of stressful events or negative circumstances; alternatively, it can exacerbate these effects.

Sociology Textbook

Now write the highlighted words in the chart according to their word form.

Nouns	Verbs	Adjectives	Adverbs

REVIEW

1. Which words in the reading passage above are the most important to know? Circle them. Explain your decisions to a partner or a small group.

2. Add five words from "The Role of Groups" on page 67 to your Vocabulary Log. Write all of the word forms each word can take and underline the suffix of each word. (Alternatively, you may add words from the Chapter Reading on pages 72–73.)

Study Tip: Create a Support System

As soon as possible, identify or create a support system: a group of people who can encourage you and advise you. They may also help you to solve problems and manage stress. People in your support community might include your family, friends, classmates, social organizations, co-workers, professors, and people in various other communities that you are a part of. Think about people in your communities who can help you. Make a list of everyone in your support system. Put the list someplace where you can see it every day. Stay in regular contact with people in your support system. Don't be afraid to ask for help when you need it.

■ Speaking Strategy

◎ *Strategy 3: Initiating Contact with Classmates*

Meeting new people in a class is not always easy. But your classmates, and even your instructors, are potentially members of your support system. You should make connections with other people so that you can get help later if you need it. You can also find a study partner or create a study group outside of class.

Don't wait for other people to come to you. Here are some ways to initiate contact with others:

- Smile and say "hello" to someone in the class who you do not know.
- Find out the names of people who sit around you.
- Try these conversation starters: *Is this the first class you've taken in this subject? What other courses are you taking? Have you taken any other classes with this instructor? Where do you live? Where are you from? What's your major?*
- Exchange phone numbers or e-mail addresses with at least two students in your class. This way, you will have someone to contact if you miss a class. You can find out what material was covered and what homework was assigned. You may even find a study partner or group this way.

PRACTICE

The next time you come to this class or to another class, try the strategies listed above to make contact with your classmates. As an extra challenge, ask someone to be your study partner, or create a study group of four to five people to meet at a specific time and place and review the material for the class.

> ### ✓ Study Tip: Use Office Hours
>
> Professors are available at certain times for "Office Hours." These hours are usually stated on a professor's course syllabus, on a class website, or on the professor's office door. "Office Hours" are times when you can see a professor without an appointment. You can use these times to ask for clarification about an assignment or lecture, or to discuss an idea for a writing assignment. Professors are happy to have students come to their office hours—most complain that students do not use them enough! However, you should never use office hours to ask a professor to repeat information from a class that you missed. Always check with another student or a study group. Professors do not like to hear these questions: "I missed class on Monday. Did you talk about anything important?" or "Could you tell me what you talked about on Monday?"

■ Reading Strategy

◎ *Strategy 3: Highlighting and Underlining a Text*

Some students don't like to write in their books. They may have been taught that it is not good to write in books, or they may hope to sell the books back to the bookstore later for some money. However, writing in your books is an important part of college life. It is a key strategy for understanding and remembering what you read. It forces you to become a more active reader. In addition to writing notes and questions in the margins, you should highlight or underline important ideas in your text.

Don't highlight or underline everything you read. You must decide what is most important to remember or to review. Highlighting or underlining too much makes it hard to separate main ideas and important facts from specific examples or less important facts. For example, if you went back to read this highlighted paragraph later, would you be able to tell what information is most important?

It's a good idea to highlight or underline the main ideas and key words in paragraphs. Remember, topic sentences are usually the first sentence in a paragraph, but they may also appear in the middle or at the end. Also, key words or special terminology related to the topic can be underlined. Finally, sometimes you will read a text looking only for information that relates to a certain topic. In that case, you might just underline information that relates to your focus.

READING STRATEGY REVIEW

Use SQ3R as you read the selection from a textbook below. Follow the same steps you used on pages 12–16 of Chapter 1. Write your questions in the margins of this reading or in your class notebook. Look for main ideas in the topic sentences.

VOCABULARY STRATEGY REVIEW

Circle new words that you think are important to know. Look at suffixes and at the words' placement in the sentences to determine the word form. Look for definition signals near new words. Use a dictionary to check the meanings of words that you are not sure about.

PRACTICE

As you read, highlight or underline what you think is the most important information.

Subcultures

In every society there are groups that possess distinctive traits that set them apart from the main culture. Groups that share in some parts of the dominant culture but have their own distinctive values, norms, language, or material culture are called **subcultures**.

Often we think we can identify subcultures on the basis of physical traits, ethnicity, religious background, geographic region, age, gender, socioeconomic or occupational status, dress, or behavior defined as deviant by society. Determining which people constitute a subculture, however, is actually a complex task that requires careful thought; it must go beyond simply including everyone who shares a particular trait. For example, using broad ethnic or racial categories as a criterion for identifying the various subcultures within the United States makes little sense. The broad racial category "Native American," for example, ignores the fact that the early residents of North America "practiced a multiplicity of customs and lifestyles, held an enormous variety of values and beliefs, spoke numerous languages mutually unintelligible to the many speakers, and

did not conceive of themselves as a single people—if they knew about each other at all" (Berkhofer 1978, p. 3).

Sociologists determine whether a group of people constitutes a subculture by learning whether they share a language, values, norms, or a territory and whether they interact with one another more than with people outside the group. One characteristic central to all subcultures is that their members are separated or cut off in some way from other people in the society. This separation may be total or it may be limited to selected aspects of life such as work, school, recreation and leisure, dating and marriage, friendships, religion, medical care, or housing. It may be voluntary, result from an accident of geography, or be imposed consciously or unconsciously by a dominant group. It could also result from a combination of these three factors.

Subcultures within the United States experience separation in different ways or to varying degrees. Some integrate themselves into certain areas of mainstream culture when possible but remain excluded from other areas of life. In general, African Americans who work or attend school primarily with whites are often excluded or feel

Sociology Textbook

excluded from personal and social relationships with them. This exclusion forces them to form their own fraternities, study groups, support groups, and other organizations. Other subcultures are **institutionally complete** (Breton 1967); that is, their members do not interact with anyone outside their subculture to shop for food, attend school, receive medical care, or find companionship because the subculture satisfies these needs. Often we find a clear association between institutional completeness and language differences. Persons who cannot speak the language of the dominant culture are very likely to live in institutionally complete ethnic communities (for example, Little Italy, Chinatown, Koreatown, Mexican barrios). Of the 750,000 Koreans living in the United States, for example, approximately 300,000 live in southern California. A large portion of these California residents live in an institutionally complete Koreatown west of downtown Los Angeles. Nevertheless, the Korean experience in the United States cannot be described by a few generalizations. For one thing, "Korean immigrants to the United States are not always from Korea. Significantly large Korean communities exist outside Korea in Siberia, Canada, Japan, and even Brazil" (Lee 1994, p. 39).

Despite the ethnic similarity among the people, Korea has been divided since 1945 into two institutionally complete subcultures: North Korea and South Korea. The people of the two Koreas have no relationship with one another (including no correspondence by mail, phone, or travel) and technically remain at war with one another. The line that separates the two people at the 38th parallel is the most heavily militarized region of the world; each side is poised to stop the other from invading. Both sides recognize their common language, ethnicity, history, and culture, and both believe in unification. Yet, despite these similarities, neither side has been able to compromise on the preferred economic or government structure, the elective process, or the appointive process for government offices.

Source: From *Sociology: A Global Perspective (with Info Trac), 5th edition,* by John Ferrante. Copyright © 2003. Reprinted with permission of Wadsworth, a division of Thomson Learning: *www.thomsonrights.com.* Fax 800-730-2215.

Sociology Textbook

▼ Reading Review and Discussion

A. Understanding the Reading

1. What are subcultures?

2. Complete the chart with information from the text:

Characteristics of Subcultures According to Most People	Characteristics of Subcultures According to Sociologists

3. According to this text, why is identifying subcultures a more complicated process than it might seem?

4. What are three factors that can result in a subculture's total or limited separation from the rest of society?

5. What does it mean for a subculture to be *institutionally complete?*

B. Applying the Reading

1. The text mentions African-American students as an example of a group that may feel excluded from the dominant culture on a college campus. Who else do you think might feel excluded on a college campus or in any school? Why might they feel excluded?

2. The text lists some ways in which African-American students might respond to feelings of exclusion. What are they? Are these responses positive or negative? Can you think of other ways in which a subculture on a college campus (or in any school) might respond to feeling excluded, either positively or negatively?

3. The text lists some examples of subcultures that are "institutionally complete." What are they? What other institutionally complete subcultures can you think of? What institutionally complete subcultures might be found on a college campus or in any other school?

C. Connecting to the Reading

1. Look back at the chart you completed in the Warm-Up section of this chapter (page 63). Would any of the groups that you are in be considered a subculture, either by people in general or by sociologists? Why? Look back at the answers you wrote in the chart under Understanding the Reading on page 74. According to which criteria might these groups be considered subcultures? If any would not be considered subcultures, explain how they do not fit the criteria.

2. What do you think are the positive and negative aspects of being a member of a subculture? Are there advantages? Disadvantages? Dangers?

■ Listening Strategy

◎ *Strategy 3: Listening for Signal Words and Phrases*

Certain words or phrases signal, or predict, what kind of information will follow. They tell us what to expect. Signal words can be used for different purposes, such as showing comparison, contrast, examples, or reasons. You don't need to write them down when you take notes, but paying attention to signal words can help you to decide what information to write down. Thinking about signal words can also help you to organize your notes later when you review; try to determine the relationship of ideas and information when you review your notes, and use signal words to explain them. Here are some common signal words and phrases to listen for.

Signal Words and Phrases	Purpose
First, Secondly, Thirdly, Next, In addition, Additionally, Also, Besides that, Furthermore, Moreover	Ordering information, adding information (especially adding similar information)
First, Second, Next, After that, Afterward, Then, Meanwhile, Subsequently, In the end	Listing ideas in time order (chronological sequence)
But, However, Nevertheless, Nonetheless, In contrast, On the other hand, Alternatively, Conversely	Showing contrasting information or ideas
Similarly, Likewise, Along those lines, In comparison	Showing similarities
For instance, For example, To illustrate, Specifically, As an example, An example of that is . . .	Showing an example
In other words, That is, That is to say, What I mean by that is . . .	Clarifying and explaining
Indeed, In fact, As a matter of fact, Interestingly, Significantly	Adding emphasis
As a result, Consequently, Thus, Therefore	Showing results or conclusions

LISTENING STRATEGY REVIEW

Prepare your paper for note-taking using either a bulleted list format or a block/paragraph format. The class is sociology. The lecture topic is "Ingroups and Outgroups." Listen for clues that indicate main ideas and important information.

PRACTICE

Listen to part of a lecture from a sociology class (Lecture 3) called Ingroups and Outgroups. You can listen to the lecture on the audiotape, or your instructor will deliver the lecture using the transcript in Appendix C of this book. Listen for information following signal words. Take notes as you listen.

EXTRA PRACTICE

Listen to the lecture again. This time, write down only the signal words and phrases that you hear. How many did you hear? What purposes do they have? Compare your answers with a partner.

▼ *Lecture Review and Discussion*

1. Find or create a study group with three to five classmates. Review your lecture notes together. What information did you write down? Did you miss any information? Help each other to fill in any blanks.

2. Review your notes with a group. Explain the main ideas of the lecture you just heard. You can take turns explaining different parts of the lecture, or you might use strategies that you used for different learning styles in Chapter 2.

3. Discuss with your groups: What kinds of examples of ingroups and outgroups were given in the lecture? What additional ingroups or outgroups can you think of? What kinds of styles, symbols, or objects are associated with them? How do these groups identify themselves?

4. With your group, write a question related to the topic of the lecture. It should be a question that you think would be interesting to discuss. (*Hint: Why* or *Do you think/agree . . . ?* are usually good question openers.) Pass your question to the group on the right. Discuss the other group's question. Keep exchanging questions with other groups until you have discussed everyone's topic.

■ Writing Strategy

◎ Strategy 3: Determining Purpose and Audience

Deciding on your purpose and audience before you start writing makes writing easier. You can select information more easily and develop a focus.

Your *purpose* is your reason for writing. What do you want your readers to think or to do? How do you want them to feel about your topic? Common purposes for writing are:

- to explore or express your feelings
- to entertain
- to inform, report, or explain something
- to argue a point, or persuade someone to do something

Your **audience** is your reader or readers. Sometimes we write with an **intended audience** in mind: a specific person (or people) whom you can easily picture. For example, when you write a letter to a financial aid officer, or you e-mail a professor about an assignment, you are writing for an intended audience. More often, you will have to do writing assignments without a clear sense of who the intended audience is. Yet, imagining an audience is still important. For some writing assignments, you can imagine a **general audience** of readers—not just your professor, but also your classmates and other readers who are interested in what you have to say but may not know the topic as well as you do.

When you have a specific audience in mind, you should think about what the readers may or may not know about your topic. You should think about your purpose: what do you want them to do or to think? Finally, you should be sure to choose the correct tone and language to address that person. You would not write to your professors, for example, in the same way that you would write to a friend. (See the study tip box on page 80 for advice on e-mailing professors.)

PRACTICE

Look at the following topics for a letter or e-mail in the left-hand column of the chart. For each one, list specific ideas that you could write about. Then list possible audiences. Finally, list possible purposes. Try to list at least two purposes for each audience. The chart has some ideas to get you started.

Topic	Specific Ideas	Possible Audiences	Possible Purposes
What I did at school last week	Gave an oral presentation and got an "A"	My parents	To show them I'm doing well in class
Problems that I had in a class or on an assignment	Failed a test	The teacher of the class	To ask for help
Problems that affect my school or a community in my school	The dorms are noisy and dirty	The Director of Campus Housing	To write a letter of complaint and ask her to help solve the problem

REVIEW: BRAINSTORMING AND CLUSTERING

Choose one of the topics from the chart. Then choose a specific idea, an audience, and a purpose. Brainstorm or cluster ideas about this topic.

_____

_____

_____

_____

Next, choose a different audience and/or purpose for the same topic. Brainstorm or cluster ideas about this topic for this new audience and/or purpose. Compare your brainstorming/clustering results. What information would you include or exclude, depending on your audience and purpose?

_____

_____

_____

_____

✓ Study Tip: Write an E-mail to a Professor/Instructor

Even though e-mail is an informal way of communication for most people, you should use more formal language and structure when e-mailing a professor or instructor.

- Always include a brief phrase in the subject line (for example: *Question about Assignment 2*).
- Start with a salutation: *Dear Professor Sweet:* (not *Hi, Diane*).
- Remind the instructor of who you are: *My name is Souren Gee, and I am a student in section 2 of your Intro to Psychology class* (not *I'm Erik*).
- Make your purpose clear: *I have a question about Assignment 2.*
- Keep your e-mail short. Don't give a long excuse about why you missed a class. Professors do not want detailed explanations of medical problems or excuses for oversleeping. Apologize and get to the point: *I was unable to attend class on Monday due to illness. May I stop by during your office hours to pick up the homework assignment?*
- Don't use slang, abbreviations, or "e-motives" such as these: thnx, see u, ;)
- Check for grammar, spelling, and typing errors before sending your e-mail.

● *Writing Task: Write an E-mail for Different Audiences and Purposes*

Write an e-mail on one of these topics. Your instructor may tell you to write either a paragraph or several paragraphs. You may use ideas from your brainstorming or clustering; you may also want to do more brainstorming or clustering.

1. Write an e-mail (or a letter) to a former teacher or to a parent. Describe what you did last week at school. Give specific examples. Then write a new e-mail or letter to a close friend. Again, describe what you did last week at school, giving specific examples. However, think about how you want this new audience to think about you. Will you include the same examples?

2. Write an e-mail (or a letter) to a professor or instructor. Tell the person about a problem that you are having. Give specific examples. Ask for advice or help. Then write a new e-mail or letter to a close friend. Again, explain your problem, giving specific examples. However, think about how you want this new audience to think about you. Will you include the same examples?

3. Write an e-mail (or a letter) to a professor or instructor, or to a senior administrative official at your school. (Or, write a letter to a student paper.) Explain a problem that you are concerned about, a problem that affects not just you but the entire community in some way. Give specific examples of the problem. Then persuade your audience that something needs to be done about this problem. If at all possible, offer some solutions. After that, write a new e-mail or letter to a close friend. Explain the same problem, but this time you don't have to persuade the reader to do something. Instead, try to entertain your reader. Find the humor in the situation, if you can.

■ Graphics Strategy

◉ *Strategy 3: Creating Pie Charts*

Pie charts can be useful ways to organize information such as statistics or percentages from surveys. Some computer programs make it easy to create pie charts. You can also draw them yourself. A pie chart often has two parts: a circle with sections (like pieces of a pie) that show percentages for each category of information, and a key. The key helps to explain information in the chart by showing what different colors or shadings mean.

Here is an example of a pie chart showing the results of a survey on what clubs or organizations students belong to on a college campus:

Participation in Student Organizations

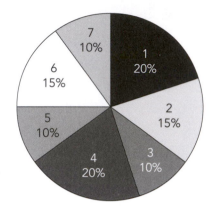

KEY
1 Academic Societies (History Club, Math Club, etc.)
2 Religious Organizations
3 International Students Organization
4 Athletic Teams
5 Political Clubs
6 Arts/Culture Club (Dramatic Society, Choir, Orchestra, etc.)
7 Do not participate in any campus organizations

PRACTICE

Alone, with a partner, or with a small group, conduct a survey on one of the following topics and create a pie chart to show your results. Explain your pie chart to the class.

1. What campus activities or organizations do students participate in?

2. What kinds of people are included in students' support systems?

3. What are the biggest challenges that students face today?

4. What are the most important problems that exist at your school?

5. What student behaviors do professors most object to?

6. What is the best thing professors think students can do to improve their grades?

7. How do students spend their "free time"?

8. Your own topic?

■ Test-Taking Strategy

◎ *Strategy 3: Answering True/False Questions*

Some people think that true/false questions are easy because they have a 50 percent chance of getting them right. However, this type of question can be tricky. There are many ways to make a statement false. Follow these steps for interpreting and answering true/false questions.

- For a statement to be true, it must all be true. If any part of the statement is false, then the whole statement is false. One incorrect word or phrase may make the statement false. Look closely at key words, numbers, and dates in the statement.
- Watch out for words like *always, all, every, none, never,* and *no.* These words can indicate generalizations, and a generalization may not be true for everyone or in every situation. Therefore, a statement with one of these words may have a greater chance of being false.
- Watch out for words like *usually, often, sometimes, may, most, many,* and *generally.* These words make general statements less extreme, allowing for exceptions. Statements with these words are more likely to be true.
- Watch out for negative words like *not* or *no.* Underline them. If you read too quickly, you may miss them. A negative word may make a true statement false.
- If you're not sure, guess. But be aware that most tests include more true items than false items. This is because true/false tests are often written to emphasize main ideas from a reading or a lecture. If you have no idea, it's safer to mark the item True.

Here are several examples of true/false test items and how they can be interpreted:

Circle **T** for true and **F** for false.

A community is always based on geographic location.   T   F

The word to watch out for in this statement is *always.* This word indicates a generalization, or an absolute statement. While it's true that some communities are defined by place (such as neighborhoods), many communities are made of people who share interests and values; some people in online communities, for example, might never even meet physically. If you can think of exceptions to a statement with *always,* the statement is likely to be false. The correct answer, then, is F.

A suffix will usually indicate the form of a word.   T   F

Hopefully you remember from earlier in this chapter that suffixes, or word endings, can tell us the form of a word. The word *usually* here is important. If you took it out of the sentence, you would be left with a generalization that sounds too extreme. Some suffixes are used for more than one word form. Therefore, a statement without *usually* would be false. Because the statement contains *usually,* it is likely be to true—it limits the claim and allows for exceptions.

PRACTICE

Use the strategies discussed to work through the following true/false test items. Be aware of which strategies you are using to answer each question.

1. Highlighting or underlining too much information makes it hard to separate main ideas from supporting details.   T   F

2. When listening to a lecture, it's not important to listen for signal words or phrases.   T   F

3. Most academic writing is done with a general audience in mind.   T   F

4. Because e-mail is so informal, it is never a good idea to contact a professor by e-mail.   T   F

5. Pie charts are generally useful for organizing statistics and percentages.   T   F

Orientation

Finding Out about Student Organizations

College campuses offer many different clubs and organizations around social, academic, or athletic interests. Joining a club is a good way to make new friends and to build your support system. It's also a good way to relieve stress. In addition, many employers like to see that students have been involved in organizations. It can be hard to find the time to join a club, especially if you work or take care of a family. However, some organizations require only a minimal commitment; some meet as infrequently as once a month. You might even be able to join an organization electronically (though e-mail or a website discussion board), participating when it's convenient for your schedule.

YOUR TASK

1. If you are currently in or near a college, find out what student clubs and organizations are on campus. If you are not currently in or near a college, use the Internet to research a college that interests you. Find out if any student organizations have websites or links. Or contact the Student Activities Center by phone or by e-mail and ask to interview someone about student organizations. Find the following information and write notes in the chart:

    What student organizations exist?

    Approximately how many students are in these organizations?

    Approximately how often/when do these groups meet?

    How can students start new organizations or clubs? What is the process?

Athletic Teams and Clubs	
Special Interest Organizations (groups that enjoy doing specific activities or talking about specific issues)	
Organizations Based on Values (religious, political, etc.)	
Student Support Groups and Services	
Social Organizations and Clubs (groups for entertainment purposes only	
Other?	

2. Compare your results with a small group or share them with the class.

3. Which campus communities would you like to join? Why?

4. Which campus communities would you <u>not</u> like to join? Why not?

▼ *Final Project*

Studying a Community, Subculture, or Ingroup

Working with a partner or a small group, decide on a community, subculture, or ingroup that you would like to study. It should be a group that you can easily find on your campus or near where you live. You will study this group to understand how it functions as a community, a subculture, or an ingroup.

1. Brainstorm possible groups to study. Then choose the one that seems the most interesting to study.

2. Think about what you know about this group. Are you members of this group yourselves? If you are not members of this group, what ideas or stereotypes do you have about this group? Brainstorm ideas about what you already know.

3. Think about things you want to know about this group. Write questions that you would like answers to.

4. Think about your audience. Who will be reading or listening to your report? What do they know and probably want to know about this group? List your ideas.

5. Think about your purpose. What do you want to do in this report? For example, do you want to describe a group that most people don't know about? Explain the problems faced by a particular group? Change people's ideas about a group? Persuade other people to help a group? Write your main purpose in one sentence.

6. Study your group. You can use one or all of these methods:

   - Observe the group. Take detailed notes on what you see and hear.
   - Interview one or more members of the group.
   - Conduct a survey among people in the group.

7. Present your findings to the class in a group presentation, or write your results in a short report. Try to use vocabulary and

ideas that you learned in this chapter. Include a pie chart if you conducted a survey. In your oral or written report, you should explain:

- What makes this group a community, subculture, or in-group? Does it fit your definition of a community or a subculture? Use information from one of the readings or the lecture in this chapter for your definition.

- How does this group define itself? (For example, does it define itself through a certain style of dress? A language or way of speaking? A geographic location? Against another group?)

- What problems or conflicts does this group experience? Are they internal conflicts (problems among members of the group), or external conflicts (problems between this group and another group)? What are the possible causes of the problems? Is the group attempting to solve them? How do you think the problems might be solved?

- What was the most interesting or surprising thing that you learned about this group? Why? Did the group challenge your expectations? Did you have an idea about this group that was either confirmed or proven incorrect?

- What is the most important thing that other people should understand about this group?

▼ *Check Your Progress*

How are you doing so far? Put a check mark in the box that best explains how you feel about your progress in each category. Be sure to ask your instructor or classmates for help if there is something that you don't understand or that you would like to review.

Topic	I understand this topic very well; I feel confident about using it again.	I understand most of this topic; I feel moderately confident.	I understand some but not all of this topic.	I don't understand this topic well; I need to review.
Key Words				
Vocabulary Strategy 3: Identifying Suffixes and Word Forms				
Speaking Strategy 3: Initiating Contact with Classmates				
Reading Strategy 3: Highlighting and Underlining a Text				
Listening Strategy 3: Listening for Signal Words and Phrases				
Writing Strategy 3: Determining Purpose and Audience				
Graphics Strategy 3: Creating Pie Charts				
Test-Taking Strategy 3: Answering True/False Questions				
Orientation: Finding Out about Student Organzations				

Which class participation tip(s) from Chapter 1 did you use?

_____

_____

Which small group participation job(s) did you do?

_____

_____

Which strategies did you use to initiate contact with classmates? Who did you contact?

_____

_____

Who are the people in your support system? Write their names, phone numbers, and e-mail addresses here:

_____

_____

What was the most important thing you learned in this chapter?

_____

_____

If you checked "do not understand" for anything in the chart on page 89, write a question about that topic:

_____

_____

Look back at the personal learning goals you set in "Getting Started" on page xxvi. What did you do in this chapter to help yourself meet those goals?

_____

_____

4 ⧚ Innovations

1. Which of the following technological inventions (or innovations) do you use? Rank them in the order of importance to you. Write 1 in front of the most important item and 6 in front of the least important.

   _____ *computer*   _____ *instant messaging*   _____ *DVD player*

   _____ *Internet*   _____ *cell / mobile phone*   _____ *other?*_____

   _____ *e-mail*   _____ *digital camera*   _____ *other?*_____

2. Compare your rankings with people in a small group. Do you agree or disagree about the most important technological innovations? Tell the group about the invention you ranked number 1. Why is it important to you? How often do you use it? How has it affected or changed your life?

3. What are some advantages and disadvantages of each invention listed above? Brainstorm ideas with your group.

4. Can you think of any non-technological innovations that have affected your life or the life of someone you know (for example, an idea? A system? A device or a tool)? List ideas with your group.

5. In your opinion, how important is technology in colleges or classrooms today? Does technology always help people to teach and to learn? Can technology sometimes make learning more difficult? Working with your group, support your opinion with specific examples. Then discuss this question with another group that has a different opinion from yours.

Key Words

Read the words in the box. You will see these key words used in this chapter. Circle the words you don't know. Use a dictionary to check the meanings. Underline suffixes that might help you to identify the word form. Then match the words to their definitions.

browse	graphics	ingenuity	links	navigate
compress	implement	innovation	multimedia	transmit

1. innovation _____   a. to send something somewhere

2. graphics _____   b. connections between Internet files

3. browse _____   c. to start using a new idea or process

4. transmit _____   d. something new; an invention

5. implement _____   e. to make something smaller

6. ingenuity _____   f. visual images

7. links _____   g. text, graphics, sound, and video together

8. multimedia _____   h. to find a way to travel or to move

9. navigate _____   i. creative skill or imagination

10. compress _____   j. to read or look at something randomly

■ Vocabulary Strategy

◎ *Strategy 4: Recognizing Technical Jargon*

Jargon is a word used to describe specialized words or terms. Different fields of study or professions may have specific jargon used by people in that field. For example, doctors use specialized terms to talk about medical conditions. Baseball players and sports reporters have specialized terms to talk about the game. Jargon can be hard to understand for people who are not in that field. Also, some words that you recognize may have a different, specific meaning in the context of a profession or field of study.

Technical jargon is one type of jargon that can be hard to understand. It is often seen in places like computer manuals, instructions for technological devices, and articles or textbooks related to the sciences. It's important to identify which terms may be used as jargon, especially if the word may have more than one meaning. Sometimes important technical words are **boldfaced** or *italicized*, but not always. Definitions for technical terms are sometimes provided. Look for words like *that is* and definition signals (see Vocabulary Strategy 2 in Chapter 2, page 38, on looking for definition signals near a word). Sometimes examples are provided to help you understand the meaning of the term: Look for example signal words like *for example, such as,* or *like*. Other terms you may need to look up in a dictionary, or decide how important they are to know. Sometimes it is not important to know every term that you see. (Review Vocabulary Strategy 1A in Chapter 1, page 6, on determining important words.)

PRACTICE

1. Look back at the words in the Key Words box. Which of these words might be technical jargon? Which words might have both a technical and a non-technical meaning?

2. Read the following passage from a textbook. Look at the highlighted words. Which ones are examples of technical jargon? Which are not? Write the words in the chart following the passage.

Innovations and the Information Explosion

At least two technological innovations are responsible for the information explosion: computers and telecommunications. Both technologies help people create, store, retrieve, and distribute large quantities of printed, visual, and spoken materials at mind-boggling speeds. Comparing the size and capabilities of the first computers with those of the present day suggests why the volume of information has increased so rapidly over the past 50 years. The computers of the 1940s weighed five tons, stood 8 feet tall and 51 feet long, and contained 17,468 vacuum tubes and 5,000 miles of wiring (Joseph 1982). Although they performed simple calculations in a few seconds, they tended to overheat and break down. Early computers also used so much power that the lights in nearby towns often failed when the machines were turned on. And, because of their size and cost, these machines were used only by the U.S. Department of Defense and the U.S. Census Bureau. Today, in contrast, a single silicon chip only a quarter-inch thick can process millions of bits of information in a second. The chip has reduced computer size and cost and has made possible the widespread use of the personal computer.

Similarly, telecommunications have increased our ability to send information quickly across space. Although the telephone, radio, and television have existed in some form for as long as 100 years, methods of rapidly transmitting clear signals have changed considerably over that time. Fiber-optic cables and satellites have replaced wire cables as the means of transmitting images, voices, and data. In 1923, the cable connecting Great Britain and the United States contained 80,000 miles of iron and steel wire (enough to circle the earth three times) and 4 million pounds of copper. It could transmit the equivalent of 1,200 letters of the alphabet per minute across the ocean. By comparison, when the capabilities of fiber optics are exploited fully, a single fiber

Sociology Textbook

the diameter of a human hair can carry the entire telephone voice traffic of the United States and transmit the contents of the Library of Congress anywhere in the world in a few seconds (Lucky 1985). This latter example is no small feat, considering that the Library of Congress houses 100 million items on 532 miles of shelves (Thomas 1992).

One software tool that has helped to increase the amount of data available at our fingertips is **hypertext**.

Anyone who has used the World Wide Web as a research tool has encountered hypertext. It allows readers to pick and choose among highlighted keywords and follow links to related documents that are stored in computers around the world. As readers select keywords and move from one linked document to another, they may wander off along tangential links, some of which may not even be remotely related to the topic at hand.

Source: From *Sociology: A Global Perspective (with InfoTrac), 5ᵗʰ edition,* by Joan Ferrante. Copyright © 2003. Reprinted with permission of Wadsworth, a division of Thomson Learning: *www.thomsonrights.com.* Fax 800-730-2215.

Sociology Textbook

Now complete the word chart. An example is provided for you.

Technical Jargon	Non-Technical Words
telecommunications	mind-boggling

REVIEW

1. Which words in the reading passage on pages 94 and 95 are the most important to know? Circle them. Explain your decisions to a partner or a small group.

2. Which of the highlighted words in the passage have definition signals nearby? How many words can you define without using a dictionary?

3. Add five words from "Innovations and the Information Explosion" to your Vocabulary Log. Write all of the word forms each word can take and underline the suffix of each word. (Alternatively, you may add words from the Chapter Reading on pages 99–103.)

■ Speaking Strategy

◎ Strategy 4A: Asking for Clarification

If you don't understand something in a group discussion, it's okay to ask for clarification. Wait until the speaker has finished speaking. Then try using one of these polite phrases:

- *What exactly do you mean by that?*
- *I'm sorry, but I'm not sure that I heard you correctly. Could you repeat that?*
- *Could you please say the last part again?*
- *Excuse me, but I didn't quite follow all of your points. When you said _____ , what exactly did you mean?*
- *I'm a little unclear about _____. Would you mind going over that again?*

◎ *Strategy 4B: Clarifying Your Ideas*

Sometimes somebody else may ask you for clarification. In that case, you can use these phrases to make your ideas more clear:

- *I'm sorry, I guess that wasn't very clear. Let me try again.*
- *What I'm trying to say is that . . . .*
- *In other words, ...*
- *Here's another way to look at it.*
- *Let me give you an example to illustrate my point.*

PRACTICE

1. Work with a partner. Ask your partner to explain a complicated subject, such as how to do a certain math problem, or how to say something in another language. Use these phrases to ask for clarification and to be sure that you understand everything. The person explaining a topic should uses phrases for clarifying ideas. Then switch roles.

2. Choose at least one of the phrases and be prepared to use it if there is something you don't understand in your discussion that follows the reading.

√ **Study Tip: Protect Your Work from Computer Disasters**

If you write on a computer, always save your work on a disk or a zip drive. That way, if your computer crashes, you will still have a copy of your work. Also be careful if you use a computer in a public space, such as the library or a computer lab. Always scan your disk for viruses before and after you use a public computer. And never leave copies of your work on public computers. Public computers are cleaned regularly, so you might not find your file saved there the next day.

■ Reading Strategy

◎ *Strategy 4: Skimming and Scanning for Patterns of Organization*

As you learned in Chapter 1, surveying a text—the first thing you should do—involves previewing it quickly. One specific way to survey a text is to scan it to understand how it is organized. Look for headings and subheadings. Headings and subheadings are like titles for sections of an article or a chapter. They tell you what that section will be about. In this section, "Reading Strategy" is a heading. "Skimming and Scanning for Patterns of Organization" is a subheading beneath it.

READING STRATEGY REVIEW

Use SQ3R as you read the selection from a Web Design manual. Follow the same steps you used on pages 12–16 of Chapter 1. Write questions in the margins of this reading or in your class notebook. Look for main ideas and topic sentences. Highlight or underline important information and key terms.

VOCABULARY STRATEGY REVIEW

Circle new words that you think are important to know. Look at suffixes and the word's placement in the sentence to determine the word form. Look for definition signals near the word. Identify technical jargon. Use a dictionary to check the meanings of important words you are not sure about.

PRACTICE

You are about to read a section from a manual on designing a webpage. Before you read, skim and scan the reading for headings, subheadings, and lists.

Understanding the Possibilities of the Web

A good cook visits many restaurants and eats many meals. Before attempting to work magic in the kitchen, the cook spends a great deal of time in the dining room to better understand what a good meal looks and tastes like. As you plan your Web site, you should do the same thing. To understand the many possibilities for communicating over the Internet, you should visit a variety of Web sites. Look for sites published by various organizations, serving various purposes, reaching diverse audiences, and using a range of technologies.

Understanding the possibilities of the Web will help you to select the best Web site functions and structures to serve your site's purposes. A personal computer connected to the Internet can be used to communicate with your audience in many ways, including the one-way communication you see in the traditional media as well as new forms of interactive and two-way communication. The Web lets you take advantage of most of the ways that human beings have invented to communicate: the human voice; images; text; sound and music; animation; motion video; and virtual reality. All these are among the possibilities you have to choose from as you plan your Web site.

Using Text

Text is not the oldest form of human communication, but it's the most efficient for many types of information. It's also what the Web began with. The inventors of the Web were looking for ways to share text files among scientific researchers around the world. These long, technical documents contained only words and numbers—no pictures, no diagrams, no pretty colors. Because text was designed from the start as a fast and efficient way to share ideas among widely scattered audiences, it travels quickly along the Internet.

The language of most Web pages is Hypertext Markup Language (HTML). This system of coding text files for retrieval and display over the Internet was invented when most of the information that was sent over the Internet was text. Many web pages are full of graphics, animation, and video and have little text, but text remains the fastest and most compact way to communicate a lot of ideas quickly. It takes advantage of the Internet as it was engineered to be used. Most Web sites use text extensively to get their ideas across.

WEB DESIGN MANUAL

This page from the Web site of a college course uses text for two purposes: to communicate the content of the news and to help users navigate and execute commands. The only graphic on this page is the college logo-type. Notice that the text is carefully designed and laid out so that it's easy to read. It uses a font that is easy for the eyes to follow. There's plenty of white space at the margins. There are no pictures to interfere with the text, which is black on a plain white background.

Reading from a computer screen is not as comfortable as reading from the pages of a book, so it's important for Web site designers to go out of their way to make the text on their Web sites easy to read.

Images

After text, images are the most frequently used form of information on the World Wide Web. Most Web pages use at least a few images, and some sites are made up almost entirely of pictures and graphics.

In the early days of the Internet, Web designers could use only small images, if they used them at all. Some browsers did not display images well. Most users' connections to the Internet were so slow that downloading a three-inch photograph might take 10 or 15 minutes. As image compression technology has improved, as browsers have matured, and as users' bandwidth has increased, images have become less of a burden to the system and so are used widely.

Even with increased bandwidth for many users, you must still consider the cost of using images on a Web page. In the time it takes typical home users to download a small photograph (about four seconds using a typical 56k connection), they could have downloaded four or five pages of single-spaced text. At the bandwidth of a typical modem, a picture is worth about 3000 words.

Multimedia

The Web is growing quickly in its ability to support communications using media other than text and static images. **Multimedia** (the term coined to refer to the range of online media available) Web elements are more accessible to more people as their bandwidth increases, and the tools for creating and publishing animation, sound, video, and other forms of interactivity are becoming easier to use. As you consider the possibilities offered by these media, take a look at the purposes and functions you listed earlier for your Web site. Can any of them be accomplished best through the use of multimedia?

CHAPTER FOUR

To be effective, multimedia elements require considerable bandwidth. Sound and video are especially hungry for kilobits. In addition, music and animations that play themselves unsolicited may annoy users. So before you plan to include multimedia in your site, think about your audience. How many of them enjoy a high-bandwidth connection? How many do you expect will upgrade by next month? By next year? The possibilities for multimedia on the Web are powerful, but only if they fit the situation of your audience and help further the purposes of your site.

Animation

In its simplest form, an **animation** is a series of still images played one after the other to give the appearance of motion and change. Animations can be used to capture the eye of a viewer or to illustrate a process. An example of the former is a banner ad on a Web site that flashes "Win $1000!" alternating with "Click here now!" The second type might include a moving diagram that shows the process of photosynthesis in a biology lesson. The first type is easy to create and takes little bandwidth to receive. The second example requires careful development and may take more time to download.

As you think about multimedia for your site, it's a good idea to browse the Web for examples of animation. Almost every site uses some sort of eye-catching animation, but few employ more complex and serious animations. For complex (but not always serious) animations, connect to the Macromedia Flash Web site at *http://www.macromedia.com/*. Flash is a program used to create complex animations. We can't print animation examples in this book, but you can view several on a short online visit.

Text can be animated, as can shapes, logotypes, drawings, and photographs. Animations can play so quickly that they are hard to see, or slowly to create a somber mood. An animation can stay in one portion of the Web page or move across it. For example, a car dealership site might feature an animation of a car speeding across the screen. An environmental site might show a moving map of the deforestation of the Amazon rain forest. A biography site might show a series of portraits, each dissolving into the next as the subject ages. An educational site might illustrate the process of changing a faucet washer through a multistep animation. How might animation help you accomplish some of the purposes of your site?

Sound

Sound is the most primitive of the means of communication. Many animals use sound to communicate what's up. Humans have been speaking to

WEB DESIGN MANUAL

one another from our beginning as humans, probably before we drew pictures and certainly before we wrote books. Music, another ancient invention, communicates feelings and moods in a different way than does spoken language. As Internet bandwidth increases and computers get better at reproducing sound, we will see more voice and music on the Web. In a culture such as that in the United States, where people spend almost half their day listening to television and radio, you cannot ignore the appeal of voice and music to this audience.

Although few sites need to use voice technology to achieve their objectives, you'll find that voice can often supplement text and images to communicate more powerfully with the target audience. For example, voice might be used on a news Web site to broadcast a press conference by a public official. In the earlier example of the animation of the washer replacement, a voice might be used to help the home repairer follow the steps one by one. A friendly voice might remind visitors to "Shoot the monkey to win a million dollars!" Clearly pronounced words and phrases can help a student learn a foreign language online.

The use of music on the Web is growing quickly. Some Web sites are all music, such as the radio stations that broadcast live and continuously on the Internet. Others play music on demand, letting you listen to your favorite sonata or popular torch song whenever you wish. To put the viewer into a relaxed mood, a soft Mozart divertimento plays on a Web site for a mountain resort. Hot jazz plays whenever you log on to a New Orleans tourist site. A university's school of music lets you listen to student compositions on its Web page.

To implement sound on the Web you use special software tools. One such tool is Macromedia SoundEdit, which records sound from the original source in a digitized form that can be transmitted over the Internet. Raw sound files are huge, requiring bandwidth of about 100k, so they must be compressed before they are used in a Web site.

Video

You can think of **video** as a series of still images that are played back rapidly so that they create a feeling of motion, accompanied by a synchronized sound track. That's how video works on television and also on the Web. Video files are even larger than sound files, so to work effectively, video files require significant compression as well as high bandwidth. These technologies are improving swiftly, and Web users increasingly will come to ex-

CHAPTER FOUR

pect to see video as part of the browsing experience. Not all Web sites need video to accomplish their objectives, but the thoughtful Web designer needs to consider the role of this most popular form of multimedia.

It's a good idea to browse the Web looking for video. Organizations such as the British Broadcasting Corporation and ABC News, for example, send a live video stream on their Web sites 24 hours a day. You might also find an online course at a university that includes video archives of guest speakers and lecturers. A manufacturer of kitchen appliances shows key product features using short video clips. You might find a live video Web cam sending video from a water hold on the African savanna to help viewers understand the daily routines of wild animals.

Virtual Reality

Virtual Reality (VR) refers to **panoramas** in which you can enjoy a 360-degree view of a location by moving the mouse as if you were moving your viewpoint. It also includes views of **objects** that you manipulate with the mouse and rotate as if they were in your hand. Producing these forms of virtual reality is fairly easy. They do not take very much bandwidth and can be useful for certain purposes. A real estate site, for example, might allow visitors to step inside the living room of a house for sale and see the view from the picture window. Then users might walk into the kitchen, zoom in on the granite countertops, and spin around to see the lovely cherry cabinets. Many automobile manufacturers give visitors a similar experience from the interior of their latest models.

This technology offers many possibilities. A museum site might provide VR displays of its pre-Colombian artifacts, which Web users can pick up, turn over, and zoom in on to see special carvings. A retailer of high-end sneakers might let potential online purchasers do the same with various models of running shoes. A course on home repair might include an object VR of a faucet valve viewable from all angles.

To find some virtual reality on the Web, a good place to start is by going to *http://www.apple.com/quicktimevr/*. To create these kinds of VR files, you take a long series of still photographs from many different angles and then combine them into a single image file. When this file is viewed with a special software plug-in, the user is presented with an experience that's close to reality. For now, at the planning stage, consider where virtual reality might help your site accomplish some of its purposes.

Source: Adapted from *Web Wizard's Guide to Web Design*.

▼ *Reading Review and Discussion*

A. Understanding the Reading

1. Who is the intended audience for this reading? (Who is it probably written for?)

2. What is the purpose of this reading? (What is the writer trying to do?)

3. What are the three main forms of information used on the World Wide Web?

4. According to the subheadings in this article, what are the four elements of multimedia used on the World Wide Web?

5. Complete the following chart with information from the reading. Two sample answers have been done for you.

Type of Web Media	Definition and/or Examples of How It Can Be Used	Advantages	Disadvantages
Text/HTML		The fastest and most compact way to communicate a lot of ideas quickly	
Animation			
Sound			Raw sound files are huge (they use a lot of bandwidth), so they must be compressed before they are used in a website. People with slow Internet connections might not be able to get sound quickly.
Video			
Virtual Reality			

B. Applying the Reading

1. Considering the advantages and disadvantages of various forms of Web design, discuss the best media elements to be used for the following types of websites:

   a student's personal website (or homepage)
   a library's website
   a movie studio's website
   a university music department's website
   a professional sports team's website
   a hospital's website
   a bank's website
   an art gallery's website

2. Look at the website for your college or institute, or for a college or institute that interests you. Which web design elements do you notice? How do they make the website easy or difficult to use? If the site does not use multimedia elements, discuss how they could be implemented and what they would look or sound like. For example, if sound were added to the website, what would it be and when would it be heard? If virtual reality were added, what panorama would viewers see?

C. Connecting to the Reading

1. Discuss a website that you have visited recently or that you use regularly. What forms of web design does it use? Does it use any multimedia elements? What do you like or dislike about this website? Is it easy to use? Discuss specific features.

2. Do you have a personal website, or do you know someone who does? How is it designed? What forms of web design does it use? Does it use any multimedia elements? Why or why not?

3. The text states: "Reading from a computer screen is not as comfortable as reading from the pages of a book." Do you agree or disagree? Do you prefer reading from websites or paper? Why? Do you think that in the future all of our reading will take place online? Would this be a good idea?

> ## ✓ Study Tip: Plan Ahead for Computer Printing Problems
>
> Professors almost never accept the following kinds of excuses for late work: "My computer printer ran out of ink." "The computer lab was closed; I couldn't print my paper." Professors also will not permit you to leave class to print a paper that is due, nor will they appreciate a late arrival to class if you were busy printing your homework. If you use a public computer and printer—or if you own one—assume that something can go wrong. Plan ahead. Never print out your paper right before class. If you have problems with a computer or printer, try to contact someone in your support group or study group to see if they can help you.

■ Listening Strategy

◎ Strategy 4: Using Abbreviations in Notes

You can take notes more quickly when you use *abbreviations* for certain words. An abbreviation is a short version of a word, or a symbol that represents a word. Some common abbreviations are provided. You might also create your own abbreviations for words that you write a lot. Just be sure that you remember what they mean!

To show time:

hour	hr	months	mos
year	yr	month	mo
second	sec	century	C
minute	min		

To show amounts or distances:

mile	mi	more than	>
miles per hour	mph	less than	<
inch	in	volume	vol
feet	ft	centimeters	cm
yard	yd	millimeters	mm

To connect ideas:

and	&	in addition	+
because	b/c	versus	vs
the same as	=	different from	≠
similar to	≈	leads to/causes	→

References to a text:

page	pg, p, pp	chapter	ch
line	l	section	sec
word	wd	number	#, no.
pararaph	par, ¶	author	au

Other words:

company	co	information	info
money	$	water	H_2O
with	w/	without	w/o
example	ex	question(s)	q (q's)

LISTENING STRATEGY REVIEW

Prepare your paper for note-taking using either a bulleted list format or a block/paragraph format. The class is Philosophy (or Ethics), and the lecture topic is "Social Inventions." When you listen to the lecture, listen for main ideas, examples, and signal words.

PRACTICE

Listen to part of a lecture from a philosophy or ethics class (Lecture 4) called Social Inventions. You can listen to the lecture on the audiotape, or your instructor will deliver the lecture using the transcript in Appendix C of this book. Use abbreviations as much as possible when you take notes.

EXTRA PRACTICE

Listen to the lecture again. This time, don't worry about getting all of the main ideas; just listen for words that you recognize from your abbreviations chart. Write as many of them as you can, as fast as you can.

▼ *Lecture Review and Discussion*

1. With a study group or a partner, review your lecture notes together. What abbreviations did you use? Can you still understand them? If you created any new abbreviations, add them to the abbreviation chart on page 107.

2. Help each other to fill in any blanks or missing information.

3. Without looking at your notes, try to explain the main ideas of the lecture you just heard. You can take turns explaining different parts of the lecture, or you might use strategies that you used for different learning styles in Chapter 2.

4. Discuss these questions with your partner or study group.

   a. What is a social inventor? How is a social inventor different from a social activist, a social contributor, or an inventor of technological/consumer products?

   b. Do you agree that after the events of September 11, 2001, people are changing their values and want to change society in some way? Why or why not? Support your reasons with specific examples.

      c. In the lecture, you heard three types of social inventions. What are they? What other examples of social inventions can you think of?

      d. What problems do you notice in society, in your community, or even at your school? What social inventions do you think could help to solve these problems? Would a social invention be enough to solve the problem, or are other types of innovations needed as well?

5. With your group, visit the website mentioned in the lecture: *http://www.globalideasbank.org*. Find one social invention that you think is a good idea and one that you don't think is a good idea. Share them with the class, giving specific reasons for your opinion.

6. Come up with a social invention of your own to solve a problem in your community or at your school. Share it with the class—or e-mail it to the Global Ideas Bank!

Study Tip: Use the Computer for Brainstorming and Freewriting

If you write slowly by hand or want to try a different way to list ideas quickly, try brainstorming at your computer. Turn the screen down, or cover it up, so that you don't worry about structure, grammar, or spelling. Then just type your ideas freely as you think about the topic.

> ✓ **Study Tip: Use Grammar and Spell Checks, but with Care**
>
> Most word processing programs offer a grammar check and a spell check feature. These are good tools to use to help you to locate potential problems. Always use them before you turn in your work. However, be aware that the grammar check is not perfect. It can help you to identify potential sentence problems (like sentence fragments), but your sentence may actually be correct—or the corrections offered may not be the best options for what you want to say. For example, sometimes a grammar check will tell you to avoid passive voice, but in some types of writing, such as lab reports, the passive voice can be used. Be careful with the spell check, too: Don't automatically change the word to the first choice that it gives you. Always look at all the options, and think about the meaning of the sentence. Be aware of word forms. Use a dictionary to be sure you are choosing the right word.

■ Writing Strategy

◎ *Strategy 4: Narrowing a Topic, Finding a Focus*

Sometimes you will have a writing topic with a specific focus. For example, you may write a paragraph or essay in answer to a question. Much of the time, however, you will be given a more general topic, which you will have to *narrow*, or make smaller, for the length of the assignment. Your focus should be more specific if you are writing a two- to three-page paper compared with a four- to five-page paper. Similarly, your focus should be more specific if you are writing a paragraph, not an essay.

To narrow a topic, start with a general concept (usually an abstract noun). Then list specific aspects of the topic. For each aspect, see if you can narrow it to something even more specific. Then look at your ideas on the paper. Which topics would be good for a one-paragraph assignment? Which would be good for a five-paragraph essay? Which would be good for a longer report? Study the example. Can you narrow this topic even further? Can you find more specific aspects?

Concept/General Topic	Specific Aspects	More Specific Aspects
Photography	35 mm Film Cameras	How to take good 35 mm pictures
	Digital Photography	How to take digital photos
		Buying a digital camera
		Pros and cons of digital vs. 35 mm cameras
		Where to buy cameras

PRACTICE

Using this format, list specific and more specific aspects for each of the following general topics. Then write a **P** next to topics that would be good for a paragraph-length assignment. Write an **E** next to topics that would be good for a five-paragraph essay. Write an **R** next to topics that would be good for a longer report.

technology	college	computers
social inventions	my school	telecommunications

REVIEW

Choose one of the topics, and a specific aspect of it, that interests you. Brainstorm or cluster ideas related to the topic. List possible audiences that you could write for, and possible purposes that your writing could have. Circle or highlight information that could be included in a paragraph or essay about this topic. In what order would you put this information? Write an outline for a possible paragraph or essay.

● *Writing Task: Write Instructions or Explain a Process*

Write instructions about how to do something or explain the process of how something works. Your instructor may ask you to write a paragraph, several paragraphs, a short essay, or a longer essay. You may be able to use ideas from the narrowing, brainstorming, clustering, and outlining you've done already. Or you may need to do more narrowing, brainstorming, clustering, and outlining. Be sure to think carefully about your audience and purpose. What do your readers already know about your topic? What do they need to know? (Refer to Chapter 7 for more information on writing paragraphs and essays.)

1. Teach your readers how to do a simple task related to something that you know how to do. (Think of talents and skills that you have. Can you make a great paper airplane? Create a webpage? Change the oil in your car?) Give step-by-step instructions on how to do this activity. Define any technical jargon that you may need to use. You may include pictures and diagrams if you like, but write the instructions so that readers could follow them if they did not have the pictures or diagrams.

2. Think of a technological device or some other invention that you use regularly—or, invent one yourself. Give step-by-step instructions on how to make it, how to assemble it, or how use it. You may incorporate lists (with numbers or bullets) if you like. Be sure to state what the invention is and describe it for your readers. Define any technical jargon that you may need to use. You may include pictures and diagrams if you like, but write the instructions so that readers could follow them if they did not have the pictures or diagrams.

3. Explain a process or a system that you are familiar with. The process could be technical (for example, how information is transferred over the Internet) or social (for example, how registration works at your school). You could also explain a social invention that you know about or that you have invented. Take your readers carefully through the process of what happens from beginning to end. Do not give instructions, do not use numbers or lists, and do not use pictures or diagrams. Rely only on your words to make the process clear.

■ Graphics Strategy

◎ *Strategy 4: Create a Cause-and-Effect Flowchart*

Flowcharts can be useful visual aids for understanding a process or sequence of causes and effects. You can take notes in a *cause-and-effect flowchart* when you read about a process. Or you can plan ideas for a paper by writing them in a flowchart first. This type of graphic can help you to think carefully about each step and to make sure that you are not leaving anything out. It can also help you to think carefully about causes and effects, since often one effect is the cause of something else.

   Here is an example of a cause-and-effect flow chart to explain the process of social inventions:

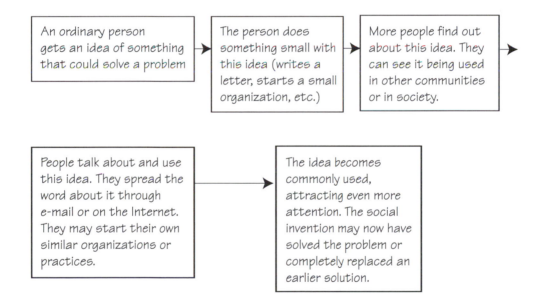

PRACTICE

1. On your own, with a partner, or with a small group, create a cause-and-effect flow chart to explain the process of designing a website. Use your notes from the Chapter Reading on pages 99–103.

2. On your own, with a partner, or with a small group, create a cause-and-effect flow chart to explain the process that you wrote about for the Writing Task.

■ Test-Taking Strategy

◉ Strategy 4: Answering Matching Questions

Matching tests can seem easy because they "give" you all the answers—you don't have to find something from memory. In a matching test, you usually match information in one column with information from the other. You may be matching parts of sentences to create true statements. Or you may be matching vocabulary to definitions; the Key Words activities in Chapters 2, 4, and 6 of this book are examples of vocabulary matching tasks.

Matching test items can be tricky, however. Follow these tips for answering matching tests.

- Read the directions! On some matching tests, you can only use each possible answer once. On others, you may be able to use the answers more than once.
- Focus only on one side. For example, look back at the vocabulary matching activity on page 92 of this chapter. Focus on the words in the left-hand column, crossing off the numbers as you make each match on the right. Or, concentrate on the definitions in the right-hand columns, crossing off the letters as you match them to the key words on the left. Don't go back and forth; you may get confused.
- Always cross off the letter, number, word, or information as you make a match. This will give you fewer items that you have to scan while you continue to make matches.

- Don't make the matches in order. Make the matches that you are sure about first. This will narrow the possible answers for the items that you are less certain about.
- Check your work again. Make sure you haven't used the same answer twice (unless the instructions permit this).
- If you are matching parts of sentences to form statements, always check to make sure the sentence makes sense grammatically. You may think the information you have matched makes a true statement, but if the sentence has grammatical errors, you have made an incorrect match.

PRACTICE

Here is one form of matching test that tests vocabulary words. Use the strategies discussed as you take this test.

_____ 1. jargon   a. titles for smaller sections of an article or chapter

_____ 2. clarification   b. short versions of words, fast ways to write them

_____ 3. subheadings   c. specialized words for specific fields and professions

_____ 4. abbreviations   d. make something smaller

_____ 5. narrow   e. the attempt to make something more clear

On page 116 is another type of matching test. This one asks you to match phrases to form complete, true statements. Use the strategies discussed to take this test. Then check the statements to be sure they are true (using strategies for true/false test questions). Be sure that they make sense grammatically too!

_____ 1. A flowchart can show   a. to organize main and supporting points.

_____ 2. Technical jargon is   b. the relationships between causes/effects.

_____ 3. Headings and subheadings help   c. can be shown in a flow chart.

_____ 4. To narrow a topic,   d. commonly found in computer manuals.

_____ 5. The process of an invention   e. start with a general concept, then list specific ideas.

Orientation

Finding Out about Computer Labs and Technical Support

If you don't own a computer or printer, you can probably use one for free at a college campus. Colleges usually have one or more computer labs or campus computing centers, where you can find different types of computers. Sometimes you need to sign up in advance for a computer.

If you have problems using your own or a public computer, you can also find help in campus computing centers or labs. There is usually a Help Desk, often staffed by students, where you can get help. Sometimes computer centers also offer special workshops and training in various computer programs. It's a good idea to take advantage of any free training if you are not comfortable with a particular program.

Finally, if you are looking to buy or sell a computer or any computer supplies, computer labs sometimes have a bulletin board where people can advertise. Some computer companies may even advertise special promotions or student discounts on hardware or software.

YOUR TASK

1. If you are currently in or near a college, find out if they have a campus computing center, computer lab, or any public computers. If you are not currently in or near a college, use the Internet to research a college that interests you. Find out if their computer center has a website. Or call the school directory and ask to be connected to a student computer center; you may be able to speak directly with someone who works at a Help Desk or to e-mail the Help Desk with questions. Find the following information and write notes:

> Is there a campus computer center or lab?
>
> How many computer centers or labs are there?
>
> Where are they located?
>
> What kinds of computers or equipment can be used?
>
> When are they open?
>
> Is there a Help Desk? If so, who works at the Help Desk?
>
> Does the lab or computer center offer any special services, like workshops or training? If so, what are they?
>
> Your own question(s): _____

2. Compare your results with a small group or share them with the class. Do the resources and services in this computer center or lab seem sufficient? Why or why not?

3. Do you or would you ever use a campus computer center or lab? Why or why not?

4. What are the advantages and disadvantages of using campus computer centers or labs? Give reasons and examples to support your opinion.

▼ *Final Project*

Evaluating or Designing a Website

OPTION ONE: EVALUATE A WEBSITE

Working with a partner or a small group, find a website that you would like to look closely at. It could be the website for your current school, for a college that interests you, for an activity or organization that interests you, for a company that interests you, or something else. You will evaluate this website to see how effectively it reaches its audience and achieves its purpose. Share your ideas with the class in an oral or written report. Your report should include answers to the following questions.

- Who do you think is the intended audience for this website?
- What do you think is the intended purpose of this website? (What does the website designer want its viewers to do, to think, to learn, or to feel?)
- What specific multimedia elements does this site use? Are they effective? Why or why not?
- Do you like the site? Why or why not? If not, how could it be improved?

OPTION TWO: DESIGN A WEBSITE

Working with a small group, imagine that you are all members of a company. Decide on a name for your company and what product you will sell, or what service you will offer. Then design a hypothetical (imagined) website for your company. Present your ideas to the class in the form of an oral or written report. Your report should include the following information.

- Who is the intended audience of your website?
- What is the intended purpose of your website? (What do you want your viewers to do, to think, to learn, or to feel?)
- What specific multimedia elements will your site use? What would these elements look or sound like? Why would you choose these elements?
- Is there a similar website out there for a company with a similar service or product? If so, would your site use some of the same strategies? Different ones? Better ones?

▼ *Check Your Progress*

How are you doing so far? Put a check mark in the box that best explains how you feel about your progress in each category. Be sure to ask your instructor or classmates for help if there is something that you don't understand or that you would like to review.

Topic	I understand this topic very well; I feel confident about using it again.	I understand most of this topic; I feel moderately confident.	I understand some but not all of this topic.	I don't understand this topic well; I need to review.
Key Words				
Vocabulary Strategy 4: Recognizing Technical Jargon				
Speaking Strategy 4A: Asking for Clarification				
Speaking Strategy 4B: Clarifying Your Ideas				
Reading Strategy 4: Skimming and Scanning for Patterns of Organization				
Listening Strategy 4: Using Abbreviations in Notes				
Writing Strategy 4: Narrowing a Topic, Finding a Focus				
Graphics Strategy 4: Creating a Cause-and-Effect Flowchart				
Test-Taking Strategy 4: Answering Matching Questions				
Orientation: Finding Out about Computer Labs and Technical Support				

Which class participation tip(s) from Chapter 1 did you use?

———————————————————————————————————————

———————————————————————————————————————

Which small group participation job(s) did you do?

———————————————————————————————————————

———————————————————————————————————————

What was the most important thing you learned in this chapter?

———————————————————————————————————————

———————————————————————————————————————

If you checked "do not understand" for anything in the chart on page 119, write a question about that topic:

———————————————————————————————————————

———————————————————————————————————————

Look back at the personal learning goals you set in "Getting Started" on page xxvi. What did you do in this chapter to help yourself meet those goals?

———————————————————————————————————————

———————————————————————————————————————

5 ॐ Health

1. Which of the following school activities cause you stress? Rank them in the order of most stressful (1) to least stressful.

_____ taking tests	_____ writing papers	_____ speaking in class
_____ giving presentations	_____ meeting new people	_____ talking to professors
_____ managing time	_____ managing money	_____ listening to lectures
_____ other? _____	_____ other? _____	_____ other? _____

2. Which of these activities do you do to try to relieve or manage stress? Circle them.

exercise	talk to friends	talk to a support group
eat	go shopping	sleep
listen to music	watch TV	other? _____

3. How many hours of sleep do you usually get each night during the week? _____

   How many hours of sleep do you usually get each night on a weekend?_____

   How many hours of sleep do you need in order to do well in school? _____

4. Discuss your responses to numbers 1 and 2 with a small group. Compare your rankings of stressful activities. Do most people feel stress from the same activities? Compare your responses to stress. Which responses do you think are healthy ways to manage stress? Which do you think are unhealthy?

5. Discuss your responses to number 3. Who gets the most amount of sleep? Who gets the least? What makes it easy or difficult to sleep?

Key Words

Read the words in the box. You will see these key words used in this chapter. Circle any words you don't know. Use a dictionary to check the meanings. Then use the words to complete the sentences. Pay attention to word form.

chronic	drowsy	impaired	nocturnal	symptoms
cite	hygiene	insufficient	sleep-deprived	variation

1. I can always tell when I'm getting a cold. My _____ include a sore throat, a headache, and a cough.

2. My textbooks for this semester are going to cost $180, but the amount of money I have is _____. I only have $120 to spend on textbooks.

3. My roommate has stayed up studying until 2:00 A.M. every night this week. Now I'm as _____ as he is— neither of us gets enough sleep when he studies so late!

4. Alessandro can never stay up past 10:00 at night. He starts feeling _____ around 9:30 P.M., even if he drinks coffee to try to stay awake.

5. Some people work better in the morning, when they feel more alert, but others are _____: They have more energy and like to do things at night.

6. The professor missed class a lot because he had _____ headaches. At least twice every month he would be in too much pain to teach.

7. Julia didn't know her vision was _____ until she saw an eye doctor. Now that she has new glasses, she can read much more clearly and quickly.

8. Germs can spread quickly on a college campus, so it's important to practice good _____ habits. Wash your hands frequently and avoid touching your eyes and nose. These simple practices can keep you from getting sick.

9. Two new studies _____ final exams as the number one cause of stress among college students.

10. Usually, Professor Cornell lectures for an hour and then leads a discussion for the last 20 minutes of class. Today, however, was a _____ from her routine—the students watched part of a film and then talked in groups.

■ Vocabulary Strategy

◎ *Strategy 5: Identifying Word Collocations and Idioms*

Some words often appear together. You can almost think of these paired or grouped words as one word. These common word combinations are called *word collocations*. Here are some common word collocations:

it's no wonder	*consistent with*	*power nap*
coined the term	*take an interest in*	*far-reaching implications*
a great deal of	*keep an appointment*	*solve a problem*

Recognizing word collocations can stop you from looking up every word in the dictionary. You can learn to recognize common word combinations and their meanings. Unfortunately, you won't see most collocations in the dictionary. A good way to learn them, then, is to write them down—maybe in a special section of your Vocabulary Log—as you come across them in your readings.

You should use the same approach to learning idioms. Idioms are words and phrases that have a special meaning. The meaning may not be clear from the individual words in a phrase; the whole phrase has a special meaning. There are dictionaries of idioms, but there are so many, it's impossible to memorize them all. Add idioms to your Vocabulary Log as you learn them.

Here are some examples of idioms and their meanings. The idioms are in the left-hand column. Cover up the right-hand column and see how many meanings you can guess.

nod off	=	fall asleep
catch some ZZZs	=	sleep
pull an all-nighter	=	stay up all night to study
a wake-up call	=	a sudden realization
a sleeper	=	something that is boring (Note: the more common meaning of "a sleeper" is a movie that seemed uninteresting at first, but quietly became popular.)

PRACTICE

Read these passages from a magazine about health and fitness. Look at the highlighted (or shaded) words. Which of them are word collocations? Which of them are idioms? Write the words in the chart following the passage. Then write what you think each idiom means.

Your Genes' Role in Depression

Why do some people bounce back from life's cruel curveballs, while others plunge into depression? The explanation may lie in genetic vulnerability. Researchers from King's College, London, and other universities tracked 847 men and women from birth to age 26, noting their reaction to stresses such as job loss and divorce. People with a variation in a gene that regulates the mood-modulating neurotransmitter serotonin were 2.5 times more likely to get depressed after a crisis. Researcher Terrie Moffitt, Ph.D., says it's too early to test for this genetic variation, but doing so might be feasible some day.

The study should reassure depression-prone people that overcoming depression is not just a matter of simply pulling yourself up by your own bootstraps, says Heather Krell, M.D., M.P.H., a professor of psychiatry at the University of California, Los Angeles, Neuropsychiatric Institute. Some people are more genetically vulnerable to depression and need professional help to boost their mood after a crisis.

Source: From *Shape.*

If Monday, Tuesday, Wednesday . . . Are Blue

What's most important for your health may not be how intensely depressed, stressed, anxious or angry you are, but how long those emotions last, one study suggests. "Staying in a negative mood for a long time can impair the functioning of your immune and cardiovascular systems," says Scott Hemenover, Ph.D., an assistant professor of psychology at Kansas State University in Manhattan. However, Hemenover adds, if your bad mood tends to linger, you can develop strategies to help yourself snap out of them faster. One is learning to think your way out of a funk. For example, if you obsess that speaking in public will lead to humiliation, "rephrase" your anxiety as a healthy part of preparing: Harness your nervous energy by rehearsing your talk and ways to cope with problems that may arise when you do it for real.

Now complete the word chart. Examples are provided.

Word Collocations	Idioms and Possible Meanings
plunge into depression	Bounce back (= recover?)

REVIEW

1. Which words in the reading passages are most important to know? Circle them. Explain your decisions.

2. Do the passages contain any jargon related to medicine and health? Write any examples of jargon here:

   _____

   _____

3. Add five words from the passages to your Vocabulary Log. Write all of the word forms each word can take. Underline the suffix of each word. (Alternatively, you may add words from the Chapter Readings on pages 130–33.)

4. List five word collocations and five idioms in a special section of your Vocabulary Log. Write the meanings of the idioms. Keep adding to this section as you encounter new word collocations and idioms in this chapter.

■ Speaking Strategy

◎ *Strategy 5: Agreeing, Disagreeing, and Consensus-Building*

When people discuss something in a group, a large part of what they do is agree, disagree, or work to come to some kind of agreement or compromise—to *build consensus*. There are many phrases you can use to introduce your ideas in these situations. Here are some of them.

Agreeing	Disagreeing	Compromising
I agree.	*I disagree.*	*Can we agree to*
(not: I'm agree.)	*I see your point.*	*disagree on this point?*
I completely agree.	*But have you*	*It looks like we don't*
You're absolutely right.	*considered . . . ?*	*see eye to eye on this*
That's correct.	*You raise an important*	*issue. However, I will*
I agree with you one	*issue. However . . . .*	*consider your view.*
hundred percent.	*I agree with you up*	
	to a point.	
	I see this very	
	differently.	
	I'm not sure that you've	
	considered all sides	

PRACTICE

1. Work with a partner. Briefly discuss a current issue or event, something that is in the news, or an issue that is affecting your school and about which people usually disagree. Use phrases from the lists as you take turns expressing your opinions. If you disagree, try to get the other person to consider your position or to agree with you.

2. Memorize or write down the phrases listed. Be prepared to use them if there is something you agree with or don't agree with in your discussion that follows the reading. Try to use phrases you don't regularly use.

> **✓ Study Tip: Visualization**
>
> If you feel stress and anxiety about a certain situation, it helps to relax, close your eyes, and imagine yourself going through the process successfully. For example, if you are nervous about talking to a professor, imagine yourself going to that professor's office hours, knocking on the door, clearly explaining your problem, and getting good advice. If you have a test to take, imagine yourself going into the room well-rested and prepared. If you have a lot of work to do, imagine yourself calmly getting everything done, turning in all of your work. If you need to give an oral presentation, imagine yourself talking to an interested group of people and hearing applause at the end.

■ Reading Strategies

◎ Strategy 5A: Identifying Facts versus Opinions

When you read anything, it's important to be able to separate *facts* (things that are true) from *opinions* (people's beliefs, attitudes, or values). Sometimes opinions are stated so firmly it seems that they are facts. Watch out for adjectives (description words); these are usually *subjective*, indicating that the statement is a person's opinion or feeling. You may also see opinions signaled with phrases like *I believe, I feel, In my opinion,* or *In _____'s view . . .*

◎ Strategy 5B: Evaluating Sources

A **source** is a text (usually an article or a book). When you write a research report, you may look at several different sources to get a lot of information—and different viewpoints—about a topic. Also, your professors may give you additional readings to supplement your text. They may request that you look at these **outside sources** to prepare for class.

However, not all sources are equally useful. Some sources may not be suitable for use in a college paper or report. For example, you read two short passages about depression and anxiety on page 125 of this chapter. Compare those passages with the chapter readings on pages 130–33. Which source would be the best one to use for a formal written report? Which would be the next best one to use? The worst?

Sources from popular magazines and personal websites are not usually the best things to use. Follow these general tips for evaluating sources.

- Is an author name given? Articles written by one or more authors are preferable to articles with nobody's name attached to them.
- Is any information about the author(s) given? Does the author have letters after his or her name, indicating an advanced degree (for example, M.D., M.A., Ph.D.)? Is the author connected to a university, a college, or a research institute?
- Does the article cite other articles and books? Is it building on the work that other people have done?
- Who is the intended audience of the article? Do titles, heading, charts, or pictures help you to answer that question?

READING STRATEGY REVIEW

Use SQ3R as you read the following two articles (Readings 1 and 2). Skim and scan headings and subheadings for patterns of organization. Write questions in the margins of the readings, or in your class notebook. Look for main ideas and topic sentences. Highlight or underline important information and key terms as you read.

VOCABULARY STRATEGY REVIEW

Circle new words that you think are important to know. Look at suffixes and the word's placement in the sentence to determine the word form. Look for definitional signals near a word. Watch out for technical jargon, word collocations, and idioms. Use a dictionary to check the meanings you are not sure about.

PRACTICE

You are about to read two articles. Before you read, think about the possible audience and purpose of each article. Are they written for similar audiences and purposes, or different ones? While you read, look for language that indicates opinions and statements that seem to be facts. (You could highlight facts and opinions in different colors). Are these articles based mostly on facts or opinions? Are they both good articles to read if you wanted to write a paper about sleep and college students?

READING 1

ACADEMIC NEWSPAPER

Professor's Crash Course Is College Students' Dream

Catching some ZZZs is as important as learning your ABCs—and may even help you learn better, says sleep researcher James B. Maas, a professor of psychology in Cornell University's College of Arts and Sciences.

He's so sure of it after 34 years of teaching that he devotes the first three and a half weeks of his popular introductory class in Psychology 101 to the importance of sleep.

Not that his class is a sleeper. Some 1,300 students line up for it each semester, making it the school's largest class offering. It's no wonder, with a standing homework assignment to nap and get more sleep.

It's really more of a wake-up call to the drowsy, reports Maas, who cites recent findings from one study showing that a college-age student who drinks one beer on five to six hours of sleep is just as impaired as a person who drinks a six-pack but has eight hours of sleep under his belt.

Maas tells students that coming to class with barely six hours of sleep is "the equivalent of lighting a match to $80," the amount he estimates it costs parents to pay for a day in the average college classroom.

He recommends going to bed at the same time on weekends and weekdays. Long an advocate of the "power nap,"—in fact, he coined the term—Maas says if you can't get a good nocturnal sleep, take a 15- to 20-minute nap.

The lesson for college students is to change their habits, says Maas.

Apparently, many of his Psych 101 students catch on quickly, according to a survey conducted last fall of 802 of his undergraduates, who reported that as a result of what they learned in Maas's class, 30 percent were getting more sleep each night and 23 percent said they were now napping more frequently from one to four times a week.

Maas discusses the details of three decades of sleep research in two new books, *The Power of Sleep: Preparing the Mind for Peak Performance*, and a second volume co-authored with Stanford University sleep researcher William Dement, MD, tentatively titled *The Stanford-Cornell Sleep Book for College Students*. Both are in the discussion stage with publishers, he says.

An award-winning professor and collaborator on a PBS prime-time special on sleep, Maas says he's probably "one of the few professors in the world" who doesn't really mind if he catches a student napping in class—though he would consider it a personal challenge to find out why. He never teaches too early in the morning or too late in the afternoon. Psych 101 is scheduled for 10 to 11 a.m.

Source: From *The Brown University Child and Adolescent Behavior Letter*.

READING 2

Relationship of Sleep Hygiene Awareness, Sleep Hygiene Practices, and Sleep Quality in University Students

Franklin C. Brown, Walter C. Buboltz, Jr., and Barlow Soper

College students are noted for obtaining insufficient sleep during the week and for sleeping long hours during the weekend. In fact, students' sleep schedules are so variable that twice as many students as people in the general population report symptoms consistent with delayed sleep syndrome. This syndrome is marked by progressively later wake-up times on nonwork or nonschool days, leading to poor job and academic performance and excessive sleepiness during the week.

Many students' sleep difficulties extend beyond voluntary schedule variations to frequent, involuntary sleep complaints. At least two thirds of college students report occasional sleep disturbances, and about one third of those report regular, severe sleep difficulties. The problem is even more evident in a recent study that found that only 11% of the students surveyed met the criteria for good sleep quality. The rest of the sample had moderate-to-severe sleep complaints. Students' poor sleep habits may, in fact, be getting worse. One study found that sleep duration decreased from about 7.5 hours per night in 1969 to 6.5 hours per night in 1989.

The apparent trend toward self-imposed sleep deprivation, irregular schedules, and poor sleep quality could have far-reaching implications. Poor sleep quality, indicated by subjective sleep ratings, sleep-onset time, sleep duration, sleep difficulties, and daytime functioning, can lead to significantly greater psychosocial distress. Examples include depression, anxiety, reduced physical health, general cognitive difficulties (e.g., poor problem solving and attention difficulties), and increased use of drugs and alcohol. Partial sleep deprivation (less than 6 hours of sleep per night) can lead to deficits in attention, concentration, memory, and critical thinking, along with increased depression, irritability, and anxiety. Even students who regularly obtain 8 hours of sleep per night but shift their sleep schedule by more than 2 hours may experience attention, concentration, reasoning, and psychomotor difficulties, as well as increased irritability, anxiety, and depression.

Unfortunately, students are often unaware of how sleep deprivation influences their cognitive functioning. Pilcher and Walters found that students who stay up all night before examinations that require critical thinking rated their performances better than those students who slept 8 hours, although the all-nighters' performance was actually much worse. The prevalence and implications of sleep difficulties warrant further exploration into underlying factors that contribute to such problems.

A group of researchers who were aware of these concerns investigated the relationship of college students' course schedules, sleep-wake variations, sleep quality, and health status. They found that students with early classes during the week had greater sleep-wake variations than those whose classes were later in the day. Furthermore, the students with more variations in their sleep schedules had shorter sleep duration and greater difficulties awakening during the week. This finding suggested that inconsistencies between students' social and academic schedules may promote variations in sleep schedules and may be a contributing factor to their sleep difficulties.

Waking at the same time each day is a key ingredient in sleep hygiene instructions, a commonly used intervention to improve sleep quality. Other activities consistent with good sleep hygiene include getting regular exer-

cise, reducing caffeine intake, taking late-afternoon naps, and curtailing alcohol consumption. Indeed, drinking coffee to improve alertness, taking naps to make up for lost sleep, and drinking alcohol to promote sleepiness are common strategies students use to counter their varying sleep schedules. In the general population, such poor sleep-hygiene practices are associated with a greater incidence of insomnia and chronic difficulties in initiating or maintaining sleep.

Although poor sleep habits in some students may be the result of late-night parties and an associated lifestyle of alcohol, drug, and tobacco use, one cannot assume that this is the case with all students. Blaming students for irresponsible sleep habits does not address the problem. Many students may be unaware that their inconsistent sleep habits can perpetuate chronic sleep difficulties; they mistakenly believe they can compensate for weeknight sleep deprivation by sleeping long hours on the weekend. In a survey of more than 900 students that assessed their knowledge of proper sleep hygiene, the average correct response rate was approximately 50%. When the researchers compared the students' knowledge of sleep hygiene with their reported sleep-hygiene practices, the researchers found that the knowledge and hygiene were positively related. On the other hand, different levels of sleep-hygiene knowledge were not found in an earlier study that compared long-term insomniacs with normal sleepers in the general population.

The weak relationship between sleep-hygiene knowledge and practices and the lack of difference between insomniacs and healthy sleepers in sleep-hygiene knowledge appear to conflict with findings in efficacy studies that suggest that teaching sleep hygiene to people with insomnia can significantly improve the quality of their sleep. In other words, it is not clear whether less knowledge about sleep hygiene contributes to students' poor sleep quality. Such ambiguous findings may suggest that there is no clear relationship. Conversely, the inconsistency may be the result of using measures with poor reliability of validity, given that there is no published psychometric information about the Sleep Hygiene Awareness and Practice Scale (SHAPS) that the researchers used in both studies. One study based insomnia ratings on a clinical interview, whereas the other measure of sleep quality was simply students' reports of sleep duration. Neither study compared sleep-hygiene scores with a standardized sleep-quality instrument.

In view of the conflicting results of previous research, we believe that a further investigation into the relationship between sleep-hygiene knowledge and practice and overall sleep quality is warranted. Such investigations may shed light on factors that contribute to poor sleep quality and help clinicians develop treatment and preventative programs to improve students' sleep quality. Thus, our purpose in making this study is twofold: (a) to analyze and report on the psychometric properties of the SHAPS and (b) to use the Pittsburgh Sleep Quality Index (PSQI), a validated sleep-quality instrument, to examine the relationship between SHAPS scores and sleep quality in college students. . . .

Source: From *Behavioral Medicine.*

▼ *Reading Review and Discussion*

A. Understanding the Reading

1. What are the first three and a half weeks of Professor Maas's class about?

2. Explain the meaning of these statements:
   a. "Catching some ZZZs is as important as learning your ABCs."
   b. "Maas tells students that coming to class with barely six hours of sleep is "the equivalent of lighting a match to $80," the amount he estimates it costs parents to pay for a day in the average college classroom.

3. According to Professor Maas, why is sleep so important for college students?

4. What are two of Professor Maas's tips for getting more sleep?

5. What evidence is given to show that Professor Maas's students have learned his lesson about sleep?

6. What is *delayed sleep syndrome?* (Reading 2)

7. What is *sleep hygiene?* (Reading 2)

8. Complete the chart with information from the second article (Reading 2):

Causes of Sleep Difficulties in College Students	Effects of Sleep Difficulties in College Students	Good Sleep Hygiene Practices

9. Explain the study conducted by Pilcher and Walters. What did their study find about students who stay up all night before examinations?

10. According to researchers, how might students' social and academic schedules negatively affect their sleep?

11. According to the authors of this study, how much do college students know about and practice sleep hygiene? What is the purpose of their study?

B. Applying the Reading

1. Professor Maas's research on sleep and performance (Reading 1) is applied to college students, who often do not get enough sleep. What other groups of people might benefit from this research? Circle the jobs below that tend to have sleep-deprived employees. Add some ideas of your own.

   airplane pilot   medical doctor   retail salesclerk

   professor   stay-at-home parent   mail carrier

   computer programmer   President of the U.S.   _____

   _____   _____   _____

2. Professor Maas recommends going to bed at the same time on weekends and weekdays. Is this good advice for college students? Why or why not? What other advice would you give?

3. Reading 2 suggests that college students may not be aware of sleep hygiene practices or the effects of poor sleep on their performance in school. How do you think students could learn more about the findings presented in this study?

C. Connecting to the Reading

1. How many hours of sleep do you get each night? Do you have trouble sleeping? If you do have difficulty sleeping, what do you think are some reasons for this? If you don't have difficulty sleeping, what good sleep hygiene habits are you practicing? Refer to reasons given in the readings and add your own reasons if you can.

2. Why do you think college students don't get enough sleep or don't sleep well? Does the first article (Reading 1) discuss enough possible reasons? Does the second article (Reading 2) discuss all possible reasons, or do you think there are others?

3. How much sleep do you need each night? How much sleep do you actually get? How do you feel when you don't get enough sleep?

4. Would you take Professor Maas's Psych 101 class? Why or why not? Give specific reasons from the first article (Reading 1) to support your opinion.

D. Evaluating the Readings

1. In the first article, what evidence is given to suggest that Professor Maas is a reliable expert on sleep and college students?

2. Who wrote the first article? Is an author name given?

3. Who wrote the second article? Is an author name given?

4. What do you think are the intended purpose and audience of Reading 1?

5. What do you think are the intended purpose and audience of Reading 2?

Study Tip: The Five-Minute Vacation

A good way to manage stress, especially during a very busy day, is to take a mental "five-minute vacation." Go away from your desk or from other people. Try to find a quiet place on campus, perhaps under a tree or in the library. Close your eyes and picture your favorite vacation place, or a place where you always feel peaceful. You can imagine yourself doing fun activities or just lying somewhere relaxing.

Another way to take a mental break is to do something different for five minutes or longer. Go to an art gallery on campus and look at a picture. Eat lunch at a different table. Browse through magazines in the student bookstore.

When you return from your mental vacation, you should feel more refreshed and relaxed, ready to complete your next task.

■ Listening Strategy

◎ *Strategy 5: Using the Cornell Note-Taking Method*

The Cornell note-taking method is a system of formatting and reviewing notes. It is a good way to review and respond to lecture notes and to study for exams.

		[Date]　　　　[Class]　　　　[Lecture Topic]
	In the left-hand margin, you will write notes about your notes when you review them.	• As you have already been doing, you will format your note-taking paper so that you have a wide left margin. In this case, leave about two inches of space on the left, and draw a vertical line to create a margin. (Or use legal-formatted notebook paper, which already has a wide left margin.)
	Write down any key words and definitions from your notes.	
	Write brief phrases that explain the type of information in each block, paragraph, or bullet point of your notes. (For example: "formatting your paper for notes.")	• Two inches up from the bottom of the paper, draw a vertical line. • Take notes in whatever format you are comfortable with: block / paragraph format, or bullet points.
	Write comments and questions. Is there any information you don't understand?	
	Can you make connections between the lecture notes and your textbook, or previous lectures?	At the bottom of the page, when you have reviewed your notes, briefly summarize the main idea of the lecture, or the main idea of the information on the page. When you are reviewing for a test, cover up the top of the page. Using only your summary, try to remember the notes that you took.

┌───┐
│ ✓ **Study Tip: Review Your Notes within 24 Hours**   │
├───┤
│   │
│ Information is most easily forgotten 24 hours after learning │
│ it. Therefore, be sure to fill in missing information from   │
│ notes and summarize notes within 24 hours after a lecture.   │
│   │
└───┘

LISTENING STRATEGY REVIEW

Prepare your paper for note-taking using either a bulleted list format or a block/paragraph format. When you listen to the lecture, listen for main ideas, examples, and signal words. When you take notes, use abbreviations whenever possible.

PRACTICE

Listen to part of a lecture from a psychology class (Lecture 5) called Causes and Effects of Stress. You can listen to the lecture on the audiotape, or your instructor will deliver the lecture using the transcript in Appendix C of this book. Use the Cornell format to write notes and summaries of each page of your notes.

▼ Lecture Review and Discussion

1. Review your notes. Write notes, questions, and key words in the left-hand margin. Write a summary of each page at the bottom.

2. With a study group or a partner, review your notes. Compare what kinds of information and questions you noted in the left-hand margin. Compare your summaries. Help each other to fill in any blanks or missing information.

3. Looking only at the summary at the bottom of each page of your notes, try to explain the main ideas of the lecture you just heard. You can take turns explaining different parts of the lecture, or you might use strategies that you used for different learning styles in Chapter 2.

4. Discuss these questions with your study group or partner:

    a. What are the three main categories of stress? Give one example of each type. Have you ever experienced any of these stressors? Can you think of other examples for each category?

    b. Thinking of "Personal Stressors," what are some examples of positive life events that can also be stressful? Have you ever experienced stress in relation to a positive life event? Share your example.

    c. What are the three phrases of response to stress according to the GAS (General Adaptation Syndrome)? Give an example of a time when you experienced one or more of these phases.

Study Tip: Manage Stress

When you are faced with a stressful situation, try one or more of these tips for managing stress:

- Make a stressful situation less stressful. Try to focus on the positive, or to think of it as potentially fun or exciting.
- Exercise. Studies show that exercise can reduce heart rate and blood pressure in the long run, improving the body's ability to cope with stress. Exercise can also help you to forget about the stressor for a while, and to regain a sense of control.
- Avoid caffeine and sugar. Drinking coffee or soda, or eating sugary snacks, can raise blood pressure, intensifying reactions to stressors or creating a feeling of stress.
- Talk about stressful situations with others. Use your friends or members of your support system. Studies show that people who have good social relationships and support systems can reduce their stress.
- Try meditation or yoga. Many communities and schools offer free or inexpensive classes in these proven stress-reducing activities.

■ Writing Strategy

◎ *Strategy 5: Summarizing and Paraphrasing*

Writing a summary of a reading, or a section of a reading, is a common activity in college classes. A **summary** is an explanation of the main points of a reading. You must use your own words and sentence structures as much as possible. A summary is always a lot shorter than the original text. This is because you only include main ideas. A summary of an article or essay might be one or two paragraphs long. A summary of a paragraph might be one or two sentences long.

There are other reasons to know how to write a summary. You may be able to use a summary as part of the introduction of a longer essay. You may be asked to write a summary to demonstrate that you read and understood a text. You can also write summaries of reading assignments to improve reading comprehension and prepare for class. Many students write brief summaries and responses to readings in a journal.

When you **paraphrase**, you explain a reading in your own words and sentence structure; however, unlike a summary, you do not reduce the length of the reading. We usually paraphrase just a sentence or two to explain a complex idea. You can think of paraphrasing as "translating" a text into different English, simplifying the language or finding your own way to say something. (For example, here is a paraphrase of the previous sentence: **When you paraphrase, you restate information using simpler terms or your own words.**)

To write a summary, follow these general guidelines:

- Write an outline of the article first, or draw a hierarchical map. Cross out points that are too detailed to include in the summary. Determine the main sections of the article and the main points of each section.
- Always mention the author and title of the original text. If you don't, your reader might think you are *plagiarizing:* representing someone else's ideas as your own. Use phrases like "The article _____ by _____ is about _____." "In her article _____, _____ says that . . ."
- Keep using verbs or phrases to remind readers that the information comes from someone else, not from you. ("As the author mentions . . . ," "According to the author . . . ," or "In the author's opinion . . .")

- Mention only the main points and possibly the most important examples. Avoid specific examples or details.
- Use your own words and sentence structures as much as possible. If you cannot find another way to explain the author's words, you can quote original phrases or sentences from the author. Be sure to put quotation marks (" ") around the author's exact words, and do not make any changes to the words inside the quotation marks.
- Use the present tense. A summary of a work of fiction or an analytical essay is in the present tense, even if it is written in the past tense. This is because the written text always exists. However, if a text describes historical or personal events in the past, use the present tense only in phrases that introduce the author's ideas or how the author gives the information. In these examples, underline the verbs in the summaries and decide why the author uses present or past tense.

Original Text (a work of fiction):

"Well, I seemed to be in the open river again, by-and-by, but I couldn't hear no sign of a whoop nowheres. I reckoned Jim had fetched up on a snag, maybe, and it was all up with him. I was good and tired, so I laid down in the canoe and said I wouldn't bother no more. I didn't want to go to sleep, of course; but I was so sleepy I couldn't help it; so I thought I would take just one little cat-nap.

"But I reckon it was more than a cat-nap, for when I waked up the stars was shining bright, the fog was all gone, and I was spinning down a big bend stern first. First I didn't know where I was; I thought I was dreaming; and when things begun to come back to me they seemed to come up dim out of last week."

Source: The Adventures of Huckleberry Finn.

SUMMARY:

In Chapter 15 of *Huckleberry Finn*, Huck floats down the river in his canoe again. He can't hear a sound, and he thinks Jim is gone or possibly dead. Feeling sleepy, he lays down for a nap. He sleeps for a long time and wakes up at night. The fog has lifted, and he doesn't know where he is. He thinks he might be dreaming. Then he starts to remember all the things that happened to him before.

Original Text (describing historical events/past opinions):

"Slavery was, above all else, an economic institution. Masters were interested in getting as much work out of their slaves as they could year round; consequently, the life of the slave was determined largely by this fact. Contrary to what some historians once believed, slavery remained a profitable and viable institution right down to the Civil War. In some regions, such as Callaway County, slavery was the most important factor in maintaining the economy."

Source: Lorenzo J. Greene, Gary R. Kremer, and Antonio F. Holland, "From Sunup to Sundown: The Life of the Slave" in *Missouri's Black Heritage* (Columbia: University of Missouri Press, 1993).

SUMMARY:

In their article "From Sunup to Sundown: The Life of the Slave," Lorenzo J. Greene, Gary R. Kremer, and Antonio F. Holland argue that slavery was an economic issue well into the nineteenth century, and that it was central to the economy in some parts of the state. They remind us that slaveholders required work out of their slaves every month of the year. Although some historians used to think otherwise, Greene et al. maintain that slavery held a great deal of economic power even until the Civil War years.

In the above summary of the nonfiction text, the verbs *argue, remind,* and *maintain* are focused on the authors, on their article (which always exists); therefore, they use the present tense. Other verbs in the article (*was, required, used to, held*) describe the institution of slavery or the opinions of people in the past.

Follow these tips for paraphrasing.

- Use a dictionary or a thesaurus to find synonyms (words with similar meanings).
- Change sentence structures. If you only replace some words, you are not really paraphrasing. Simplify complex sentences. Combine simple sentences to make them longer or complex. Change the order of information in the sentence. Change active voice to passive voice; change passive to active.
- Try to paraphrase without looking back at the original text. This can force you to find your own words or sentence structures.

Then compare your paraphrase with the original and check for accuracy. Don't leave out or change any of the information.

- Imagine you are writing for a reader who is a little younger than you, or who is completely unfamiliar with this information. Imagining this audience can force you to simplify language and ideas.
- Check your paraphrase for grammar and style.

When you write a summary, you can also use paraphrasing techniques. Here is an example of an unsuccessful summary of one of the two short articles on page 125:

> The most important thing for your health is probably not how extremely depressed, stressed, anxious, or mad you are, but how long those emotions continue, according to one study. Staying in a bad mood for a while can hurt your immune and cardiovascular systems, one expert says. This expert is an assistant professor of psychology at Kansas State University in Manhattan. But if your bad mood continues, there are some things you can do to snap out of it more quickly. One way is to think your way out. As an example, if you keep thinking that speaking in public would be embarrassing, instead think that your anxiety is a healthy way to prepare. Use your nervous energy by practicing your speech and the methods of coping with problems that may come up when you actually give the speech.

Compare the summary with the original article. The summary is unsuccessful because it is too long. A summary should significantly reduce the amount of information from the original. This summary also does not tell us where the information is from. Finally, the summary uses too many of the original writer's words and sentence structures; the writer has not paraphrased well enough. It is not enough to replace some words here and there; entire sentence structures need to be changed.

Here is a better summary of the short article.

> In the *Shape* magazine article entitled "If Monday, Tuesday, Wednesday . . . Are Blue," the author discusses research that suggests the duration of negative moods or stress is more significant than the intensity of the emotions during those unhappy times. The author cites an expert who mentions that although being stressed for a long period of time can have negative effects on one's physical health, there are skills you can use to get out of a bad mood. One way is to think positively about a stressful event, turning anxiety into positive energy and imagining ways to deal with the stress.

PRACTICE

1. In one paragraph, summarize one or both of the Chapter Readings on pages 130–33. Or, in several sentences, summarize a section of one of the Chapter Readings.

2. Looking back at the Chapter Readings on pages 130–33, find three interesting or important sentences from each one. (These may be topic sentences that you already underlined or highlighted.) Write a paraphrase of each one.

● *Writing Task: Write a Summary*

Following the guidelines above, write a summary (one paragraph or several paragraphs—your instructor will tell you) of an article.

1. Find a short article in the newspaper, in a magazine, or on the Internet that is related to the general topics of stress, sleep, or health. Write a clear, one-paragraph summary of the article so that other students in your class can understand the main ideas without reading the article themselves.

2. Find a short article in the newspaper, in a magazine, or on the Internet that is related to the general topics of stress, sleep, or health. In one paragraph, summarize the article so that other students in your class can understand the main ideas. Then, in a separate paragraph (or essay), write a focused response to the article. State an opinion about the article or about the topic that it is discussing. Use examples from the article, your experience, or your observations to support your opinion. (***Review:*** You may need to do some brainstorming or clustering to get ideas for your response section. Organize your examples in the order of importance, and think about your audience. Will you need to define any key terms? Does your article, or your response paragraph, use any technical jargon that should be explained?)

3. Write an opinion essay (or a letter to the editor in a student newspaper) about a health-related issue affecting students (for example: *sleep, stress, anxiety, depression*). Find one or more articles on

this topic. Summarize the article(s) in your introduction or in a separate section of your essay. Use paraphrased or quoted examples from the articles to support your opinion. (***Review:*** You may need to do some brainstorming or clustering to get ideas for your response section. Organize your examples in the order of importance, and think about your audience. Will you need to define any key terms or jargon?

✓ Study Tip: Eat a Balanced Diet

When you are in college, it can be easy to forget how to eat right. Your schedule may be strange or inconsistent. You may have a class at lunchtime or three classes in a row. It's easy to skip meals or to eat unhealthy snacks and junk food when you're rushing from one place to the next. Sugar and caffeine can give you more energy temporarily, but this energy doesn't last, and you are likely to feel even more tired later. Try to eat three meals a day, or to eat a healthy snack (like fruit) every few hours. Eat a later breakfast or an early dinner if your schedule conflicts with "normal" meal times.

■ Graphics Strategy

◎ *Strategy 5: Creating Bar Graphs*

Bar graphs, like pie charts, can be useful visual aids for organizing data from surveys. You might find bar graphs in textbooks and articles. You might create them for presentations and reports. Some computer programs make it easy to create bar graphs. You can also draw them yourself. A bar graph has two main parts: a vertical axis (a line going up and down on the left side) and a horizontal axis (a line going left to right at the bottom). In fact, the vertical and horizontal axes look like the margins you created when you prepared your lecture note paper for the Cornell note-taking method.

vertical axis |

horizontal axis

Here is an example of a bar graph showing the results of a student survey on what activities people do to relieve stress. The numbers on the vertical axis show the percentage of people who were surveyed. The information on the horizontal axis describes each activity.

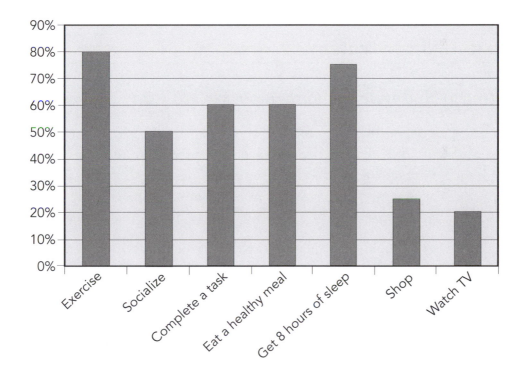

PRACTICE

Alone, with a partner, or with a small group, conduct a survey on one of the following topics and create a bar graph to show your results. Explain your bar graph to the class.

1. Which school activities cause the most stress?

2. What things do people do to relieve or manage stress?

3. What positive events in people's lives cause the most stress?

4. Why don't students get enough sleep?

5. What strategies do people use to get more sleep?

■ Test-Taking Strategy

◎ *Strategy 5: Answering Paragraph-Length Essay Questions*

Some test questions will ask you to write an answer in your own words. You may be asked to write one or more paragraph-length answers to questions about the text, a lecture, or several texts or lectures together. These questions are challenging because you not only need to know the material, but also how to organize your ideas quickly. Follow these tips for answering paragraph-length essay questions:

- Predict possible essay questions. Review your reading notes and lecture notes to look for possible topics. Did your professor or the test emphasize a topic? Make connections between topics? Also look at discussion questions at the end of readings or chapters in a textbook. Outline possible paragraph-length responses.
- Understand how to structure a paragraph. Your response should have a topic sentence, specific examples, and a concluding sentence. (See Chapter 1 and Chapter 7 for a reminder of paragraph structure.)
- Manage your time. Allow time for planning and brainstorming in the beginning. Use brainstorming, clustering, and outlining strategies. Allow a few minutes for proofreading at the end.

- Read the question carefully. Circle key words. Watch out for these types of words that will tell you how to answer the question or organize your ideas:

    compare (focus on similarities)
    contrast (focus on differences)
    describe (give specific details, create a mental picture of something)
    define (give a meaning or definition)
    discuss or explain (give a detailed answer with supporting reasons/examples)
    enumerate (list examples, points, or reasons)
    evaluate (write about both positive and negative aspects of the topic)
    illustrate (explain something by providing examples)
    summarize (give an overview of the main ideas)
    trace (explain the process of something)

- Watch out for small words like *and, or, no,* and *not.* These words can expand or narrow what you need to talk about in the answer. For example, *and* means that you must write about two or more items that are given to you; *or* means that you have a choice. *No* and *not* can further limit a topic by telling you to exclude some kinds of information or ideas.
- Be sure you are answering the question. Try using part of the question in your topic sentence. (You can paraphrase it later if you have time.)
- Write as neatly as you can. If you are given lined paper, skip every other line (double space) when you write. This makes your writing easier for someone to read and grade; it also makes it easier for you to find and correct mistakes when you proofread.
- To prepare, predict questions and practice writing. Look through your reading assignments and lecture notes. Write possible questions about the material. Find information from your notes and write a paragraph response to each possible question. Then try writing the paragraph again from memory.

Here is a sample test question, followed by an explanation of how you might interpret it and prepare a paragraph-length response:

Define "sleep hygiene" and explain how college students
perceive and practice it.

For this question, you are asked to do two things: define and explain. After reviewing the reading in this chapter, it should be fairly easy to produce a definition. If you can't remember, thinking about your knowledge of the word *hygiene* (a key word in this chapter) should help you to guess the meaning. After that, you are asked to explain—to give a detailed answer with supporting examples. Also, notice the second *and* in this topic. You must explain how college students view (or what they know about) the concept as well as their behavior. Compare that topic with this one:

Define "sleep hygiene" and explain how college students perceive or practice it.

In this version, *or* narrows the topic. You may discuss college students' perception of sleep hygiene or how they try to use sleep hygiene, but you need not discuss both.

Some paragraph-length questions may ask for your opinion. You can probably use examples from texts or lectures in the class to support your overall opinion. You may also be free to bring in examples from your own observations or experience. Here is an example of a question in which you could incorporate things that you've read or heard in a lecture with your own opinion.

Enumerate the major causes of stress for high school students
compared with college students.

Notice that this question asks you to do two things: enumerate (list examples) and compare (compare causes of stress in two different levels of education). Here is a sample answer to the last question.

The major causes of stress for high school and college students are similar, but they are more extreme among college students and therefore produce more stress. The top three stressors are homework, personal relationships, and sleep-deprivation. In high school, more homework is given each year, and the pressure increases to do well in order to graduate and hopefully get into a college. However, homework is even more stressful in college because there is more of it, it is more advanced, and there is less guidance about how to do it. Moreover, college students are usually responsible for managing their own time—teachers and parents are not constantly telling them to do their work. Secondly, personal relationships can be stressful in high school. Many teens begin to date at this time, and to form new social groups based around their growing interests. As boyfriends, girlfriends, and social groups come and go, these changes can create stress. In college, these same dynamics of dating and socializing occur, but with the added workload of homework and possible outside employment, the stress intensifies. Alternatively, college students may find they don't have time for dating and socializing, and this, too, can cause stress. Finally, sleep-deprivation causes a great deal of stress at both levels of education, yet again is felt more acutely among college students. High school students may be sleep-deprived as they test boundaries, staying out late at night with friends and tasting freedom for the first time. They also may do many extracurricular activities (such as theatre or sports) that involve late night performances or travel to other places, which can take its toll on students. Among college students, however, sleep deprivation intensifies. Many college students pull all-nighters; there may even be pressure to do so in a dorm or group living situation. Also for students not living at home, the noise of a shared living space, or the habits of a nocturnal roommate, can inhibit a good night's sleep. In addition, many college students work a part-time job to help pay their tuition bills; it is not uncommon for a student to go to school all day and go to work in the evening, or to work during the day and attend some classes at night. All of these stressors can negatively impact learning, but the consequences of stress are even more serious for college students, where more tuition money has been spent and their future job prospects may depend on their getting good grades.

PRACTICE

Use the strategies discussed to help you answer one or more of these paragraph-length essay questions. Be sure to circle key words that can help you to organize your ideas.

1. Trace the process of consensus-building in a group discussion.

2. Define "idioms" and "word collocations." Explain why they are easy or difficult to learn. Support your opinion with specific examples.

3. Compare or contrast the Cornell note-taking method with another note-taking method you have learned or practiced. Which method is more effective? Why?

4. Evaluate the advantages and disadvantages of using a bar graph to show data in an oral or written report. Describe a project for which you might use a bar graph.

Study Tip: Talk to a Professional to Reduce Stress, Anxiety, or Depression

It's easy to feel overwhelmed or stressed-out in college. Anxiety and depression are common among students, but students may not always recognize the symptoms. Additionally, if you are an international student, you may be experiencing stress associated with "culture shock," or adjusting to a new culture. Psychologists and counselors are usually available on college campuses or through referrals to help students. They can talk to you about your feelings and screen you for anxiety or depression. Many students find that talking to a professional even just once can help to reduce some stress. A psychologist, counselor, or therapist can become a "quiet" part of your support system. The information you talk about is confidential, and you do not need to tell anyone that you are working with a professional to help manage your stress.

Orientation

Finding Out about Campus Health Centers

Every college has a health center on campus. At the health center, you can see a doctor or a nurse. You may be able to receive psychological counseling services. Some health centers even have nutritionists to help you to lose weight or eat healthy foods. They may sponsor health programs, classes or workshops. For example, some students attend workshops to learn about the signs of depression, to quit smoking, or to manage stress.

YOUR TASK

1. If you are currently in or near a college, find out if there is a health center. If you are not currently in or near a college, use the Internet to research a college that interests you. Find out if their health center has a website. Or call the school directory and ask to be connected to the health center. You may be able to get recorded information or speak with a receptionist. Find answers to the following questions and write notes:

   Is there a health center?

   > If there is, where is it located?

   > If there is not, where do students go if they need health services?

   When is the health center open?

   Who works in the health center? (How many doctors? Nurses? Counselors?)

   How do you make an appointment? Is it possible to see someone without one?

   Does the health center offer any special programs, classes, or workshops? If so, what are they?

   Are all the health services free for students? If not, how do students pay for them?

   Your own question(s): _____

   _____

2. Compare your results with a small group or share them with the class. Did you find any information that surprised you?

▼ *Final Project*

Designing a Stress-Management Program for Students

Most people would agree that students have a lot of stress in their lives. How do you think students could manage stress more effectively? Should they do things to change their personal behaviors and attitudes? Should they learn more ways to cope with stress? Should schools and workplaces be more involved in helping people to manage stress?

Working with a partner or a small group, design a program to help students learn to manage stress. Share your ideas with the class in an oral or written report. Use vocabulary, strategies, and information from this chapter. Your report should include answers to the following questions:

- What are the most common causes of stress among students?
- How do most students try to cope with stress?
- What could students do to manage stress? How could they learn these strategies?
- How could a school do more to help students manage stress? (Be creative!)

Your report might also include:

- A survey and bar graphs to show some of your survey data. (You may be able to use information from your Graphics task in this chapter.)
- Ideas from articles that you read. You could use the articles in this chapter, an article you found for the Writing Task in this chapter, or additional sources. You could summarize one or more articles or paraphrase some ideas. Be sure to tell people where you found the information.

▼ *Check Your Progress*

How are you doing so far? Put a check mark in the box that best explains how you feel about your progress in each category. Be sure to ask your instructor or classmates for help if there is something that you don't understand or that you would like to review.

Topic	I understand this topic very well; I feel confident about using it again.	I understand most of this topic; I feel moderately confident.	I understand some but not all of this topic.	I don't understand this topic well; I need to review.
Key Words				
Vocabulary Strategy 5: Identifying Word Collocations and Idioms				
Speaking Strategy 5: Agreeing, Disagreeing, and Consensus-Building				
Reading Strategy 5A: Identifying Facts versus Opinions				
Reading Strategy 5B: Evaluating Sources				
Listening Strategy 5: Using the Cornell Note-Taking Method				
Writing Strategy 5: Summarizing and Paraphrasing				
Graphics Strategy 5: Creating Bar Graphs				
Test-Taking Strategy 5: Answering Paragraph-Length Essay Questions				
Orientation: Finding Out about Campus Health Centers				

Which class participation tip(s) from Chapter 1 did you use?

_____

_____

Which small group participation job(s) did you do?

_____

_____

What was the most important thing you learned in this chapter?

_____

_____

If you checked "do not understand" for anything in the chart on page 155, write a question about that topic:

_____

_____

Look back at the personal learning goals you set in "Getting Started" on page xxvi. What did you do in this chapter to help yourself meet those goals?

_____

_____

6 ≶ Work

1. Read the following list of life *values*, or beliefs, related to work and lifestyle. Which ones are the most important to you? Check the top five values for you and then rank them in order of priority (1 is the most important to you, 5 is the least).

    _____ a. Location: Being able to live where I want to live.

    _____ b. Enjoyment: Enjoying my work, having fun doing it.

    _____ c. Friendship: Working with people I like and being liked by them.

    _____ d. Loyalty: Being loyal to my boss and peers; having their loyalty in return.

    _____ e. Family: Having time with my family.

    _____ f. Leadership: Being truly influential.

_____ g. Achievement: Accomplishing important things.

_____ h. Self-realization: Doing work that is personally challenging and that will allow me to realize the full potential of my talent.

_____ i. Wealth: Making money and becoming financially independent to do what I want to do.

_____ j. Expertise: Being a pro (skillful), an authority in what I do.

_____ k. Service: Contributing to the satisfaction of others; helping people who need help.

_____ l. Social Service: Contributing to my country, my community, or to the world at large.

_____ m. Prestige: Being seen as successful; becoming well known, perhaps; obtaining recognition and status.

_____ n. Security: Having a secure and stable position.

_____ o. Power: Having the authority to approve or disapprove proposed courses of action; making assignments, initiating projects, and controlling allocation of resources.

_____ p. Independence: Freedom of thought and action; being able to act in terms of my own time schedule, work style, and priorities.

_____ q. Aesthetics: Contributing to the truth, beauty, and culture of life.

_____ r. Morality: Performing by a standard of personal, professional, and social ethics.

Source: From _The Lotus and the Pool: How to Create Your Own Career._

2. Compare your work values with people in a small group. Are your values similar or different? Explain your priorities to the group.

3. Have you ever had a job that you hated, or job that seemed to not be a good fit for you? Describe your worst job experience to the group.

4. Now that you have heard what everyone in the group values most in a job or a workplace, and you have heard about their worst job experiences, what jobs or professions do you think would be most suitable for each person? Brainstorm ideas, then share them with the class.

Key Words

Read the words in the box. You will see these key words used in this chapter. Circle the words you don't know. Use a dictionary to check the meanings. Underline suffixes that might help you to identify the word form. Then match the words to their definitions.

aptitude	compensate	equilibrium	monetary	prospective
attributes	discrimination	labor	productive	wages

1. aptitude _____   a. related to money

2. labor _____   b. balance, proportion

3. discrimination _____   c. potential; likely to become in the future

4. attributes _____   d. work

5. wages _____   e. to pay someone, or to make up for an imbalance

6. productive _____   f. talent or natural ability

7. equilibrium _____   g. capable of producing or making something

8. prospective _____   h. qualities or characteristics

9. compensate _____   i. payment for work or services

10. monetary _____   j. to treat someone unfairly because of their race, gender, socioeconomic class, or some other category

■ Vocabulary Strategy

◎ Strategy 6: Using Synonyms to Define Words and Expand Vocabulary

As explained in Chapter 2, definitions of unfamiliar vocabulary words can sometimes be indicated by definition signals near the words. One type of definition signal is a *synonym*. Synonyms are words with identical or very similar meanings. Even if you already understand the meaning of a word, it's a good idea to look for synonyms as a way to expand your vocabulary. You can look for synonyms in the same paragraph or passage as a word. Often synonyms appear one right after another, in a list form. Sometimes they appear in nearby sentences; writers like to find different words with the same meaning to make their writing more varied and interesting. You can also look for synonyms in a thesaurus. You can purchase a thesaurus in book form or use one online. Two good ones are *www.thesaurus.com* and *www.visualthesaurus.com*.

PRACTICE

1. Reread the key words in the box on page 159. Use a thesaurus to find possible synonyms for each one. Write the synonyms beneath each key word.

2. Read the following passage from a popular career guidance book. Look at the highlighted (or shaded) words. Then look for their synonyms in nearby sentences or paragraphs, or in the same sentence. Watch out for idioms and word collocations; these can be synonyms too! Write the synonyms in the chart following the passage. Then use a thesaurus to look up additional synonyms for each word. (Be sure that they are all in the same word form.)

The Ten Keys to Success are:

1. Curiosity: being eager to know and learn; always showing interest and giving special attention to the less obvious; always being the person who says, "I want to know more about . . ."
2. Decisiveness: arriving at a final conclusion or making a choice and taking action; making decisions with determination, even when you don't have all of the information you think you need.
3. Perseverance: having passion, energy, focus, and the desire to get results. Motivation, persistence, and hard work are all aspects of drive.
4. Empathy: demonstrating caring and understanding of someone else's situation, feelings, and motives; always thinking about what it's like to walk in someone else's shoes.
5. Flexibility: being capable of change; responding positively to change; being pliable, adaptable, nonrigid, and able to deal with ambiguity.
6. Follow-through: always closing the loop and taking the next step; honoring your word by doing what you said you would do and being professional in your communication and approach.
7. Humor: viewing yourself and the world with enjoyment; not taking life or yourself too seriously; being amusing, amused, and, at times, even comical.
8. Intelligence: thinking and working smartly and cleverly; being sharp in your dealings; "not reinventing the wheel"; planning before acting; working efficiently and focusing on quality over quantity.
9. Optimism: expecting the best possible outcome and dwelling on the most hopeful or positive aspects of a situation; subscribing to the belief that "the glass is half full" rather than half empty.
10. Respect: remembering that it's just as easy to be nice; protecting another person's self-esteem; treating others in a considerate and courteous manner.

Which of these keys are among your strengths? Which of the ten are among your weaknesses? Self-awareness—the ability to recognize a feeling as it happens—is really the foundation for understanding yourself. If you are not sure how self-aware you are, ask several people whom you trust which of these ten keys they believe are your strengths, and which are not. Again, while no person possesses all ten of these keys in equal amounts, each of them can be developed and improved.

Source: From *I Don't Know What I Want, But I Know It's Not This: A Step-by-Step Guide to Finding Gratifying Work.*

Now complete the word chart. Two examples are provided for you.

Word or Phrase	Synonymous Word or Phrase	Additional Synonyms?
know interest	learn special attention	comprehend, understand ?

REVIEW

1. Which words in the reading passage are most important to know? Circle them. Explain your decisions.

2. Does the passage contain any idioms or word collocations? If so, write them here:

   Idioms: _____

   _____

   Word Collocations: _____

   _____

3. Add five words from the reading passage to your Vocabulary Log. Write all of the word forms each word can take. Underline the suffix of each word. (Alternatively, you may add words from the Chapter Reading on pages 169–73.)

4. Add any new idioms or word collocations you found to that section of your Vocabulary Log.

☑ **Study Tip: Avoid Negative Non-Verbal Language**

Your body language—what you say without using words—communicates a lot about your attitude toward a job or a class. Your employer or your professor may notice your body language and get a certain impression of you. Avoid these non-verbal behaviors that signal the wrong message: *yawning, sighing, rolling your eyes, looking out the window, crossing your arms in front of your chest, and putting your head down on the desk.* These behaviors send the message that you are bored, do not like the class, or do not care about learning the material.

■ Speaking Strategies

◎ *Strategy 6A: Giving a Formal Presentation*

At some point in your college education, it is very likely that you will be required to give a formal oral presentation for a class. This is good practice for oral presentations that you may need to do at a job someday. For people who enjoy public speaking, a formal presentation is not necessarily a stressful event. But for people who do not enjoy public speaking (which is most people!), or for people who do not feel entirely confident about speaking English, a formal presentation can be a large source of stress.

The best way to succeed in a formal oral presentation is to be as prepared as you can be. Follow these tips for preparing for—and delivering—an oral presentation:

Preparing for the Presentation

- Write your notes out in large handwriting on index cards, or print them out in large font. Make them easy to see and easy to follow. Remember that people need more time to follow information given orally. You might want to mark places in your notes where you can pause.

- Practice! Practice alone in a room, more than once. Use the notes that you will use during the actual presentation so that you become familiar with them. Time yourself. Do you have enough material? Too much? Are you speaking too quickly or too slowly?

- Try out your presentation on a friend or a member of your support system. Ask him or her to tell you if anything is unclear, if you are speaking at a good speed, if you should pause anywhere.

- Consider opening your presentation with something that will get people's interest, just as you might in a paper: maybe a short personal story (about your interest in the topic, or your research process), or an interesting/surprising fact or quote. If you can perceive that your audience is interested, or if you can make them laugh, this will relax everybody, especially you.

- Consider dressing a little more professionally for your presentation. This can give you confidence; it can also send the message to your audience that you take your work seriously.

Delivering the Presentation

- Greet your audience. Give your name (if your audience does not know it) and state the topic of your presentation. This will give you a chance to hear your voice in the room. If you are very nervous, you might also write the topic on the board. This will give you a moment to take a few deep breaths.

- Focus on giving information and ideas clearly to others, not on what others may be thinking about you. Remember that people really want to hear what you have to say. Think of your audience—including your professor—as being there to learn from you.

- Use signal words like "first, second, next" in the presentation so that people can follow your points.
- Speak slowly. Most people speak too quickly when they are nervous. It is better to speak more slowly, even if it feels unnaturally slow. It is harder for an audience to get information by listening compared to reading. If you think you are likely to speak too fast, ask a friend in the audience to give you a specific gesture to remind you to slow down.
- Try to speak loudly, toward the back of the room.
- Make eye contact with your audience as much as possible. Don't read your notes word for word. If it is too scary to look at people's faces, speak to imaginary people beyond the back row, or speak to the back wall. This will at least keep your words and your face focused on your audience, not buried in your notes.
- Try to avoid distracting non-verbal behaviors, like pacing back and forth, shifting from one leg to the other, or playing with a pen or part of your clothing. If you are speaking at a podium (a special table to hold your notes), rest your hands gently on top of it, or keep them relaxed at your sides. Never chew gum.
- Have a clear end to your presentation. Summarize your main points, leave the audience with questions to think about, or say, "Thank you" or "This concludes my presentation" to signal that you are done speaking. Don't just look at the professor and say, "That's it."

◎ *Strategy 6B: Using Visual Aids in a Presentation*

Sometimes you will be required to use a *visual aid* in a presentation; sometimes it may be optional. Visuals help your audience to follow your information. Visual aids could be graphs (pie charts or bar graphs, for example), pictures (copies or photographs), or computer screens with website. A visual aid could also be a simple outline of your main points (on an overhead projector, a computer screen, or a handout). In addition to helping to make your points clear, a visual aid can make you less nervous by giving your audience something to focus on besides you! Consider using visual aids even if they are not required. However, use them carefully. Follow these general tips.

- Be sure that your visual aid is clear and readable. Any writing or images should be large enough for people to read from the back of the room. Likewise, photocopied handouts of text or images should be clear and readable.
- If your visual aid is on paper and you think it may be too small for some people to see, pass it around the audience. Don't hold it up and hope that it is visible.
- Use the visuals. Don't just point at a projection screen or poster, and don't let them sit there unexplained. Talk about each visual, point out key features, read aloud from it.
- If your visual is on display (on a poster or a screen), be careful not to stand in front of it.
- Don't turn your back on the audience to talk about your visual; your words may not be heard. Try to stand just to the side of the visual and point to it with one arm, turning only slightly.

PRACTICE

Work with a small group. Plan a short (one to five minutes) presentation on a topic that you know well. It might be about an activity you do, a hobby you have, or a job you have (or have had in the past); you should not have to do research for this. Prepare a visual aid as well: an outline of points, a picture, a chart, or an image. Then deliver your presentation for this small group, incorporating the advice given. Give each other feedback on the presentation when you are done. What was good about the presentation? How could it be improved?

✓ Study Tip: Use Positive Non-Verbal Language

Just as negative body language can signal a lack of interest in the class or the material, positive body language can send the opposite message: interest, enthusiasm, and a desire to learn! Practice these non-verbal behaviors in class: *sitting up straight, looking attentive, sitting near the front of the class, taking notes, nodding your head once in a while, smiling, raising your eyebrows to show interest.*

■ Reading Strategies

◎ *Strategy 6A: Identifying Word References*

Referring words are certain words that refer back to words, phrases, or ideas stated in a previous sentence. There are three main types of referring words:

> Pronouns: *he, she, it, they; him, her, them; his, hers, its, theirs*
>
> Demonstrative Adjectives: *this, that, these, those*
>
> Relative Pronouns: *who, whose, which, that, where*

When you are aware of these types of words, you can identify nouns or noun phrases—the *referents*—and improve your reading comprehension. For example:

> *Loyalty: being loyal to my boss and peers; having their loyalty in return*

referring word = *their*; **referent** = *my boss and peers*

> *Friendship: working with people I like and being liked by them*

referring word = *them*; **referent** = *people I like*

PRACTICE

Choose one paragraph or a short passage in the Chapter Reading on pages 169–73. Look for examples of the three types of referring words and circle them. Look for the word referents and underline them. The referent may be a word, a phrase, or an entire sentence. Draw an arrow to connect the word reference and the referent. Compare your results with a partner.

◎ *Strategy 6B: Making Inferences*

When an idea is *implied* in a reading, it is not directly stated. The reader must *infer*, or guess, the idea. Making inferences helps you to be an active reader; it is a way of responding to the text. You can write your inferences in your notes, or you can think of them in your head as you read. Here is an example of a statement with an implied meaning:

Almost any job has its benefits. "At least I don't have to take it home with me," "It's only five minutes away," and "It pays the bills" are some of the advantages people identify in their otherwise uninteresting, tedious, or unrewarding work.

Possible inference: For practical reasons, many people stay in jobs they don't like.

This statement is not directly stated, but we can understand it from the information given: the examples of "benefits" people list are all practical details, and the adjectives listed to describe their work are all negative.

READING STRATEGY REVIEW

Use SQ3R as you read the following excerpt from an economics textbook. Skim and scan headings and subheadings for patterns of organization. Write questions in the margins of the reading or in your class notebook. Look for main ideas and topic sentences. Highlight or underline important information and key terms as you read. Look for statements of fact versus opinion.

VOCABULARY STRATEGY REVIEW

Circle new words that you think are important to know. Look at suffixes and the word's placement in the sentence to determine the word form. Look for definition signals near a word. Watch out for technical jargon, word collocations, and idioms. Identify synonyms in the reading or find synonyms of important words in a thesaurus.

PRACTICE

You are about to read an excerpt from an economics textbook. As you read, watch out for referring words; be sure to check for their referents to be sure you are understanding the reading. Are there some ideas that are not stated but that come to your mind as you read? Make inferences as you read, and write them down in the margins or in your notes.

CHAPTER 19

Earnings and Discrimination

In the United States today, the typical physician earns about $200,000 a year, the typical police officer about $50,000, and the typical farmworker about $20,000. These examples illustrate the large differences in earnings that are so common in our economy. These differences explain why some people live in mansions, ride in limousines, and vacation on the French Riviera, while other people live in small apartments, ride the bus, and vacation in their own backyards.

Why do earnings vary so much from person to person?

SOME DETERMINANTS OF EQUILIBRIUM WAGES

Workers differ from one another in many ways. Jobs also have differing characteristics—both in terms of the wage they pay and in terms of their nonmonetary attributes. In this section we consider how the characteristics of workers and jobs affect labor supply, labor demand, and equilibrium wages.

Compensating Differentials

When a worker is deciding whether to take a job, the wage is only one of many job attributes that the worker takes into account. Some jobs are easy, fun, and safe; others are hard, dull, and dangerous. The better the job as gauged by those nonmonetary characteristics, the more people there are who are willing to do the job at any given wage. In other words, the supply of labor for easy, fun, and safe jobs is greater than the supply of labor for hard, dull, and dangerous jobs. As a result, "good" jobs will tend to have lower equilibrium wages than "bad" jobs.

For example, imagine you are looking for a summer job in a local beach community. Two kinds of jobs are available. You can take a job as a beach-badge checker, or you can take a job as a garbage collector. The beach-badge checkers take leisurely strolls along the beach during the day and check to make sure the tourists have brought the required beach permits. The garbage collectors wake up before dawn to drive dirty, noisy trucks around town to pick up garbage. Which job would you want? Most people would prefer the beach job if the wages were the same. To induce people to become garbage collectors, the town has to offer higher wages to garbage collectors than to beach-badge checkers.

Economists use the term **compensating differential** to refer to a difference in wages that arises from nonmonetary

Chapter 19

characteristics of jobs. Compensating differentials are prevalent in the economy. Here are some examples:

- Coal miners are paid more than other workers with similar levels of education. Their higher wage compensates them for the dirty and dangerous nature of coal mining, as well as the long-term health problems that coal miners experience.
- Workers who work the night shift at factories are paid more than similar workers who work the day shift. The higher wage compensates them for having to work at night and sleep during the day, a lifestyle that most people find undesirable.
- Professors are paid less than lawyers and doctors, who have similar amounts of education. Professors' lower wages compensate them for the great intellectual and personal satisfaction that their jobs offer. (Indeed, teaching economics is so much fun that it is surprising that economics professors get paid anything at all!)

Human Capital

As we discussed in the previous chapter, the word *capital* usually refers to the economy's stock of equipment and structures. The capital stock includes the farmer's tractor, the manufacturer's factory, and the teacher's blackboard. The essence of capital is that it is a factor of production that itself has been produced.

There is another type of capital that, while less tangible than physical capital, is just as important to the economy's production. **Human capital** is the accumulation of investments in people. The most important type of human capital is education. Like all forms of capital, education represents an expenditure of resources at one point in time to raise productivity in the future. But, unlike an investment in other forms of capital, an investment in education is tied to a specific person, and this linkage is what makes it human capital.

Not surprisingly, workers with more human capital on average earn more than those with less human capital. College graduates in the United States, for example, earn almost twice as much as those workers who end their education with a high school diploma. This large difference has been documented in many countries around the world. It tends to be even larger in less developed countries, where educated workers are in scarce supply.

It is easy to see why education raises wages from the perspective of supply and demand. Firms—the demanders of labor—are willing to pay more for the highly educated because highly educated workers have higher marginal products. Workers—the suppliers of labor—are willing to pay the cost of becoming educated only if there is a reward for doing so. In essence, the difference in wages between highly educated workers and less educated workers may be considered a compensating differential for the cost of becoming educated.

Ability, Effort, and Chance

Why do baseball players in the major leagues get paid more than those in the minor leagues? Certainly, the higher wage is not a compensating differential. Playing in the major leagues is not a less pleasant task than playing in the minor leagues; in fact, the opposite is true. The major leagues do not require more years of schooling or more experience. To a large extent, players in the major leagues earn more just because they have greater natural ability.

Natural ability is important for workers in all occupations. Because of heredity and upbringing, people differ in their physical and mental attributes. Some people are strong, others weak. Some people are smart, others less so. Some people are outgoing, others awkward in social situations. These and many other personal characteristics determine how productive workers are and, therefore, play a role in determining the wages they earn.

Closely related to ability is effort. Some people work hard, others are lazy. We should not be surprised to find that those who work hard are more productive and earn higher wages. To some ex-

tent, firms reward workers directly by paying people on the basis of what they produce. Salespeople, for instance, are often paid as a percentage of the sales they make. At other times, hard work is rewarded less directly in the form of a higher annual salary or a bonus.

Chance also plays a role in determining wages. If a person attended a trade school to learn how to repair televisions with vacuum tubes and then found this skill made obsolete by the invention of solid-state electronics, he or she would end up earning a low wage compared to others with similar years of training. The low wage of this worker is due to chance—a phenomenon that economists recognize but do not shed much light on.

How important are ability, effort, and chance in determining wages? It is hard to say, because ability, effort, and chance are hard to measure. But indirect evidence suggests that they are very important. When labor economists study wages, they relate a worker's wage to those variables that can be measured—years of schooling, years of experience, age, and job characteristics. Although all of these measured variables affect a worker's wage as theory predicts, they account for less than half of the variation in wages in our economy. Because so much of the variation in wages is left unexplained, omitted variables, including

Chapter 19

ability, effort, and chance, must play an important role.

AN ALTERNATIVE VIEW OF EDUCATION: SIGNALING

Earlier we discussed the human-capital view of education, according to which schooling raises workers' wages because it makes them more productive. Although this view is widely accepted, some economists have proposed an alternative theory, which emphasizes that firms use educational attainment as a way of sorting between high-ability and low-ability workers. According to this alternative view, when people earn a college degree, for instance, they do not become more productive, but they do *signal* their high ability to prospective employers. Because it is easier for high-ability people to earn a college degree than it is for low-ability people, more high-ability people get college degrees. As a result, it is rational for firms to interpret a college degree as a signal of ability.

The signaling theory of education is similar to the signaling theory of advertising discussed in Chapter 17. In the signaling theory of advertising, the advertisement itself contains no real information, but the firm signals the quality of its product to consumers by its willingness to spend money on advertising. In the signaling theory of education, schooling has no real productivity benefit, but the worker signals his innate productivity to employers by his willingness to spend years at school. In both cases, an action is being taken not for its intrinsic benefit but because the willingness to take that action conveys private information to someone observing it.

Thus, we now have two views of education: the human-capital theory and the signaling theory. Both views can explain why more educated workers tend to earn more than less educated workers. According to the human-capital view, education makes workers more productive; according to the signaling view, education is correlated with natural ability. But the two views have radically different predictions for the effects of policies that aim to increase educational attainment. According to the human-capital view, increasing educational levels for all workers would raise all workers' productivity and thereby their wages. According to the signaling view, education does not enhance productivity, so raising all workers' educational levels would not affect wages.

Most likely, truth lies somewhere between these two extremes. The benefits to education are probably a combination of the productivity-enhancing effects of human capital and the productivity-revealing effects of signaling. The open question is the relative size of these two effects.

CASE STUDY
The Benefits of Beauty

People differ in many ways. One difference is in how attractive they are. The actor Brad Pitt, for instance, is a handsome man. In part for this reason, his movies attract large audiences. Not surprisingly, the large audiences mean a large income for Mr. Pitt.

How prevalent are the economic benefits of beauty? Labor economists Daniel Hamermesh and Jeff Biddle tried to answer this question in a study published in the December 1994 issue of the *American Economic Review.* Hamermesh and Biddle examined data from surveys of individuals in the United States and Canada. The interviewers who conducted the survey were asked to rate each respondent's physical appearance. Hamermesh and Biddle then examined how much the wages of the respondents depended on the standard determinants—education, experience, and so on—and how much they depended on physical appearance.

Hamermesh and Biddle found that beauty pays. People who are deemed to be more attractive than average earn 5 percent more than people of average looks. People of average looks earn 5 to 10 percent more than people considered less attractive than average. Similar results were found for men and women.

What explains these differences in wages? There are several ways to interpret the "beauty premium."

One interpretation is that good looks are themselves a type of innate ability determining productivity and wages. Some people are born with the attributes of a movie star; other people are not. Good looks are useful in any job in which workers present themselves to the public—such as acting, sales, and waiting on tables. In this case, an attractive worker is more valuable to the firm than an unattractive worker. The firm's willingness to pay more to attractive workers reflects its customers' preferences.

A second interpretation is that reported beauty is an indirect measure of other types of ability. How attractive a person appears depends on more than just heredity. It also depends on dress, hairstyle, personal demeanor, and other attributes that a person can control. Perhaps a person who successfully projects an attractive image in a survey interview is more likely to be an intelligent person who succeeds at other tasks as well.

A third interpretation is that the beauty premium is a type of discrimination, a topic to which we return later.

Source: Adapted from *Principles of Microeconomics, 3rd Edition,* by N. Gregory Mankiw. Copyright © 2004. Reprinted with permission of South-Western, a division of Thomson Learning: *www.thomsonrights.com.* Fax 800-730-2215.

▼ *Reading Review and Discussion*

A. Understanding the Reading

1. How much does a doctor in the United States usually make? How much does a farmer make?

2. According to the reading, what factors may explain why earnings vary so much from person to person? List at least five.

3. Explain some of the key terms used in the reading. Complete the chart with information from the reading.

Term	Meaning	Examples
compensating differential		
human capital		
natural ability		
effort		
chance		

4. Explain the difference between the human-capital view of education and the signaling view of education. According to these views of education, what would happen if the level of education were increased for all workers? Use information from the reading to complete the chart.

View of Education	Explanation	Possible Effect of Increasing Educational Levels for All Workers?
Human-Capital View		
Signaling View		

5. How might beauty, or attractiveness, explain why people have different levels of income? Briefly explain the three interpretations mentioned in the article.

B. Applying the Reading

1. Can you think of other jobs that pay a lot for dirty, dangerous, or undesirable work? List them here:

   _____

   _____

   Would you want to do any of these jobs? Why or why not?

2. Can you think of other jobs, besides teaching, that pay lower wages because the "nonmonetary characteristics" are satisfying? List them here:

   _____

   _____

   Would you want to do any of these jobs? Why or why not?

3. In your opinion, which of these jobs might put a high value on beauty, or attractiveness? Circle the jobs that might have higher demand for employees who are attractive.

server in a restaurant	salesclerk in a fashionable clothing store
computer programmer	medical doctor
lawyer	automobile mechanic
electrician	secretary/administrative assistant in an office
dental hygienist	manager of a hotel

   Other? _____

   _____

4. Can you think of jobs where natural ability or talent might lead to higher wages? List them here:

_____

_____

5. Can you think of jobs that reward effort with higher wages (paying people on the basis of how hard they work or what they produce)? List them here:

_____

_____

6. Can you think of jobs that might pay higher wages because of chance? List them (or the chance circumstances) here:

_____

_____

C. Connecting to the Reading

1. What are the highest-paying jobs or professions where you come from? What are the lowest paying? Why do you think these jobs pay so much or so little?

2. In your hometown or your native country, do people with more education always earn more money? If not, give examples of people who earn more money than people with a higher level of education. What jobs do they do? Why do you think they earn more money?

3. In the section on "Compensating Differentials," the writer gives two examples of jobs that might be offered at a beach: checking for beach-badges or collecting garbage. The garbage collectors earn higher wages, but the beach-badge checkers have a more pleasant job. Which of these two jobs would you prefer? Why?

In general, would you choose a job that has more pleasant working conditions or a job that pays a lot more money? Why?

4. Do you believe that more attractive people earn more money or have more job opportunities? Why or why not? Explain one of the three interpretations given in the article as your reason, or give a reason of your own. Add examples from your experience or observations if possible.

5. Do you feel that movie stars or professional athletes are paid too much money? Why or why not?

6. Do you know someone who has experienced discrimination in the workplace (for example, someone who was denied a job or who earned less money because of his or her race, gender, or some other reason)? Explain what happened. What do you think was the reason for this discrimination?

D. Evaluating the Reading

1. Which of these statements from the reading do you think are facts? Which are opinions?

    a. *Professors are paid less than lawyers and doctors, who have similar amounts of education.* (Circle one: Fact / Opinion / Not sure)

    b. *Professors' lower wages compensate them for the great intellectual and personal satisfaction that their jobs offer.* (Circle one: Fact / Opinion / Not sure)

    c. *Indeed, teaching economics is so much fun that it is surprising that economics professors get paid anything at all!* (Circle one: Fact / Opinion / Not sure)

2. Look closely at the three statements in question 1. Do you think that these statements are true for all professors or teachers? Do you think that all educators are happy with their lower wages because of the personal satisfaction they get from the work? Why or why not?

3. What other factors might account for differences in wages? Can you think of any that are not mentioned in the reading?

Study Tip: Balance Work and School

Many students work part-time while going to college. Some even work full-time! If you can afford it, you should work as few hours as possible to give yourself more time to focus on school. Ideally, school should be your main job. If you do need to work, try to use your commuting time or your breaks to review readings or notes. For example, while waiting for a bus to work, you could review vocabulary words or formulas on flash cards. If possible, try to find a job that does not require a lot of mental exertion. Sometimes a job that involves physical labor or repetitive tasks can help keep your mind free to memorize information for a test or to review ideas from a reading.

■ Listening Strategy

◎ *Strategy 6: Organizing Notes into a Numeric Outline*

	Date Class Topic: "How to Write Lecture Notes in a Numeric Outline"	
	I. When to Use Numeric Outlines	
	A. A numeric outline is an organized system of numbers and letters that	
	shows the hierarchy of information (main points, subordinate points,	
	and examples).	
	B. Can you take notes in this format?	
	1. Sometimes a lecture is very well-organized. Main and subordinate	
	points are clearly given, and you can take notes using an outline	
	format.	
	2. It is not always a good idea to take notes in this format, however.	
	3 If the lecture is not well-organized, you might be too busy trying to	
	fit information into the outline and could miss some information.	
	C. Can you review notes in this format?	
	1. Creating a numeric outline is an excellent way to review lecture notes	
	later.	
	a. You can take your block or bullet point notes, or your Cornell	
	note-taking format, and put it into a numeric outline.	
	b. This process will force you to see the relationships between ideas	
	and to identify main ideas versus supporting examples.	
	c. Copying the information into a new format will also help you to	
	remember it better.	

	II. How to Write Numeric Outlines
	A. Use a consistent system of numerals, letters (capital, lower-case), and numbers to show main ideas and subordinate points/examples.
	1. Use roman numerals (I, II, III, IV, V, etc.) for main categories of information.
	2. Use capital letters (A, B, C, D, etc.) for smaller topics.
	3. Use numbers (1, 2, 3, 4, etc.) for main points or ideas within each topic.
	4. Use lower-case letters (a, b, c, d, etc.) for small points or examples beneath main ideas.
	B. Indent each subordinate point beneath the previous one. If you are typing your notes into an outline, indent subordinate points one tab, or ten spaces. If you are writing them by hand, indent about a half inch for each subordinate point.

LISTENING STRATEGY REVIEW

Prepare your paper for note-taking using a bulleted list format, a block format, or the Cornell note-taking format. The class is American History (or American Studies); the lecture topic (Lecture 6) is The American Dream: Myth or Reality? When you listen to the lecture, listen for main ideas, examples, and signal words. When you take notes, use abbreviations whenever possible.

PRACTICE

Listen to part of a lecture from an American History (or American Studies) class. You can listen to the lecture on the audiotape, or your instructor will deliver the lecture using the transcript in Appendix C of this book. After you listen, review your notes and rewrite them into a numeric outline format.

EXTRA PRACTICE

Listen to the lecture again, and this time try to take notes in a numeric outline form as you listen. How easy or difficult was it to do?

▼ *Lecture Review and Discussion*

1. Review your notes. Rewrite them into a numeric outline format.

2. Compare your numeric outline with a partner or a small group. Compare what kinds of information you assigned roman numerals, capital letters, numbers, and lower-case letters. Do you agree on the hierarchy of information? Help each other to fill in any blanks or missing information.

3. Try to explain the main ideas of the lecture you just heard. You can use the summary at the bottom of your original note-taking paper if you used the Cornell method, or recall the main categories from your numeric outline. You can take turns explaining different parts of the lecture, or you might use strategies that you used for different learning styles in Chapter 2.

4. Discuss these questions with your study group or partner.
   a. What is the "American dream"?
   b. Do you think that the American dream is a myth or a reality today? Give an example of someone you know or have heard of, or an example of a movie, that shows how the American dream is a myth or a reality. Do you believe it is possible for someone to come to this country with very little money (or to start out in this country with very little), work hard, and become very successful?

    c. Think of additional examples of people who may be excluded from the American dream.

    d. Think of additional negative aspects of the American dream.

    e. Is the "American dream" unique to the United States? Or do you think it is present in other countries and cultures too? Support your opinion with specific examples.

✓ Study Tip: Be a Professional Student

Even though you are paying for your education—the school is not paying you wages—it's a good idea to act professionally when interacting with faculty, administrative staff, and even fellow students. It is good practice for the "real world" later. And it never hurts to make a good impression on someone. You never know when that person will be in a position to offer you a job lead or even a job! Acting and dressing professionally can also help you to stay focused on school. Think of yourself as reporting to work, even when you are going to the library to study. Log the hours that you work. Stick to a schedule. Ask your professors for "performance reviews"—check in during office hours to ask how you are doing in their class and if there is anything that you can improve.

■ Writing Strategies

◎ *Strategy 6A: Using Persuasive Language*

Much of the writing that you do in college will express your personal opinion about something. You might give your opinion about an issue or about something that you read. You will then need to support your opinion with specific reasons and examples in order to persuade (or convince) readers to consider your view. These skills will be useful later in the workplace, where you may need to present your opinion or ideas and persuade people to do the following kinds of things: take action, give you money, solve a problem, or buy something, to name a few. Even applying for a job requires skill in the "art of persuasion"—you are selling yourself on paper when you write a resume or a cover letter.

In various writing assignments in this book, you have practiced the structure of persuasive writing: giving an opinion and supporting it with reasons and examples. In addition to structure, some verbs and phrases are especially persuasive. Here are some common ones.

Persuasive Phrases to Introduce Ideas	Persuasive Verbs
I would argue that	*argue*
It is necessary that . . . . / It is imperative that	*must, should, have to*
Under no circumstances should	*must not, should not*
I urge people to . . . . / I implore you to	*urge, implore*

◎ *Strategy 6B: Considering Opposing and Alternative Views*

Another way to make your writing more persuasive is to consider **opposing views** (the opinions of people who may have the opposite idea from you) or **alternative views** (the opinions of people who may have different perspectives). Thinking of your audience and purpose will help you to find the other views. In your writing, you can do these things with opposing or alternative views.

Acknowledge them (mention that they exist).

> Use these phrases: *Some people feel / believe . . . .*
>
>   *A concern that some people may have is . . . .*
>
>   *It's important to mention that . . . .*
>
>   *Those who disagree would argue that . . . .*
>
>   *My opponents would point out that . . . .*

Refute them (explain why this opposing or alternative view is not the best, and why your position is the better one).

> Use these phrases: *While they raise a good point, this idea is not practical.*
>
>   *While it may be true that . . . , the reality is that . . . .*
>
>   *There is not enough evidence to support this view.*
>
>   *While my opponents raise a good point, they neglect to mention that . . . .*
>
>   *What they fail to see is that . . . .*
>
>   *This may be true. However, ...*

PRACTICE

1. Work with a partner. Think of an issue that you can disagree about. It could be controversy in the news or an issue affecting your school or community. Take different positions. State your opinion. Acknowledge each other's viewpoint, then refute it with your own opinion and reasons. Continue your dialogue (or debate) as long as you can. Use the phrases listed above.

2. Work with a small group. Imagine that you are a company. Think of a product that you might produce or a service that you could offer. (Note: You could continue your work from Chapter 4, page 118, in which you were asked to imagine you were a hypothetical company designing a website). Think of your audience

(or market) for this new product or service. Brainstorm reasons why people should buy your product. Then brainstorm objections or alternative views that your audience might have about this project. Now go around to other groups and try to sell your product or service.

● *Writing Task: Write a Cover Letter, a Proposal, or a Persuasive Essay*

Following the guidelines, write a persuasive letter (one or more paragraphs), proposal (one or more paragraphs), or essay. Your instructor will tell you how long your assignment should be.

1. Find a job that you are interested in. It could be a job at your school or in your community. It could be a job in a field or a company that interests you. It could be a real job, or you can imagine one. In one paragraph or more, write a cover letter to this prospective employer. Explain why you are the most qualified person for this job. Mention any specific experience that relates to this job. Mention personal attributes or aptitudes that are well-suited to this job, and give at least one specific example to show why this attribute or aptitude describes you. Use persuasive language. Consider one or more possible objections this employer might have, and refute them. (For example, would the employer worry about your lack of experience or training? Give reasons and evidence to show why these are not things the employer should be worried about.)

2. Think of a problem that affects your campus, your community, or your workplace. Think of possible causes and effects of this problem. Think of who is responsible for the problem. Think of possible solutions for the problem. (Have any solutions already been attempted? Were they effective or ineffective? Do you have a better solution?) Finally, think of who you could write to with a proposed solution. (One person? An entire community?) What objectives might they have to your solution? Write your proposal

in the form of a letter to one person, a letter to the editor for a newspaper, or an open letter to a community. Define the problem and propose one or more possible solutions. Use persuasive language. Consider possible opposing and alternative views, and refute them.

3. Think of a problem that affects working people in this society or in your native culture (for example: discrimination, overwork, not enough vacation time, unhealthy workplaces, labor laws, etc.). Think of possible causes and effects of this problem. Think of who is responsible for the problem. Think of possible solutions for the problem. (Have any solutions already been attempted? Were they effective or ineffective? Do you have a better solution?) Finally, think of possible objections or alternative views that people might have about either the problem or the solution. Write a formal essay (a minimum of five paragraphs) that explains the problem and proposes one or more possible solutions. Use persuasive language. Consider possible opposing and alternative views, and refute them. Your instructor may ask you to do library or Internet research for this assignment. If you do, you may use your sources to help explain the problem, or you may use them as opposing or alternative views that you will respond to.

■ Graphics Strategy

◎ *Strategy 6: Creating Tables*

Tables, like pie charts and bar graphs, can be useful visual aids for organizing data from surveys. You can also use them to organize notes from readings or lectures; this book has presented many different tables as graphic organizers in the Post-Reading Discussion sections. Finally, you are likely to find a lot of tables of data when you read textbooks and academic articles.

Some computer programs make it easy to create tables. You can also draw them yourself. A table is similar to a bar graph in some ways: You are presenting information both horizontally and vertically. A table is made up of columns (vertical) and rows (horizontal). The far-left column is similar to the vertical axis of a bar graph. It presents categories of information. The top row is similar to the horizontal axis of a bar graph. It also presents categories of information. These are called "headings," and they often appear in **boldface**. Facts or statistics (numbers, percentages) or other data are listed in the table. You read a table both vertically and horizontally to find the statistic for each category. The table lets you compare data in various categories.

Here is an example of two tables comparing the average income for students graduating from colleges compared with those graduating from high school. Each table compares incomes over a ten-year period, from 1990–2000. One table focuses on men, the other on women.

Median Annual Income of Year-Round, Full-Time Workers 25 Years Old or Over, by Level of Education Completed and Sex: 1990–2000

Men			Women		
Year	High School Graduate	Bachelor's Degree	Year	High School Graduate	Bachelor's Degree
1990	$26,653	$39,238	1990	$18,319	$28,017
1991	26,779	40,906	1991	18,836	29,079
1992	27,280	41,355	1992	19,427	30,326
1993	27,370	42,757	1993	19,963	31,197
1994	28,037	43,663	1994	20,373	31,741
1995	29,510	45,266	1995	20,463	32,051
1996	30,709	45,846	1996	21,175	33,525
1997	31,215	48,616	1997	22,067	35,379
1998	31,477	51,405	1998	22,780	36,559
1999	33,184	52,985	1999	23,061	37,993
2000	34,303	56,334	2000	24,970	40,415

Source: From U.S. Department of Education, *Digest of Education Statistics* (Washington, DC: National Center for Education Statistics, 2003), Table 381.

DISCUSSION AND PRACTICE

1. Discuss these questions with a partner or a small group: Would it be possible to put information from these tables into a bar graph? What would it look like? Would it be possible to put information from these tables into a pie chart? Why or why not?

2. Study the information in the table. What inferences about can you make from this data? Write at least three inference statements. (Hints: What does the table tell us about the income of high school graduates compared with college graduates? What does it tell us about people's income over a ten-year period? What does it tell us about men's income compared with women's income?)

3. Alone, with a partner, or with a small group, conduct a study on the following topic and create a table to show your results. Explain your table to the class.

   Topic: How many students work part-time while going to school? Full-time? How many do not work? Show results for men and for women. You could also show results for international students, non-international students, or students in other categories.

■ Test-Taking Strategy

◎ *Strategy 6: Writing Timed Essays*

Some tests—especially midterm (mid-semester) and final exams—may require you to write an entire essay. You may also be required to write a timed essay as a placement test for the appropriate level of English class when you first enroll in a college. Timed tests are usually 50 to 90 minutes long. Sometimes you may be asked to write an entire essay about a topic or information directly related to a specific course's readings or lectures. You may be asked to read a passage from a text and write an essay about it. In your first and second years of college, however, longer essay topics may be more open-ended; they are often designed to test whether or not you can quickly focus on a topic and organize a clear, coherent, well-developed essay.

If you are a non-native English speaker, timed writing may be more challenging for you because you may need more time to find the words that you want or to check your essay for errors. However, there are some strategies you can use to do well on timed essays. In addition to using strategies for paragraph-length essay questions (see page 148), you can follow these tips for longer essay questions.

Planning the Essay Exam

- Manage your time well. Allow plenty of time for planning/brainstorming, writing, and proofreading. If you have an hour to write an essay, spend 10–15 minutes planning/outlining, 30–45 minutes writing, and the rest of the time proofreading. If you have 90 minutes, spend 15 minutes planning, 60 minutes writing, and 15 minutes proofreading and editing. If you finish early, don't leave the room! Use the time to go over your essay again.
- Underline key words in the essay topic that will help you to plan an essay. (See the list of key words for essay exams on page 148 of Chapter 5.) Choose an appropriate organizational pattern to fit the key words in the topic.
- A five-paragraph essay (see Chapter 7) is usually a good length for a timed essay. Think in "threes." When you brainstorm, can you find three ideas that might become body paragraphs or topic sentences? Can you find three examples or details for each paragraph?

Writing the Essay Exam

- Be sure you are really answering the question. Use the phrasing from the essay topic in the introduction, thesis statement, or topic sentences. Turn a question into a statement.
- Answer the question completely: Address all parts of it.
- Skip every other line (double space) as you write. This will leave room to make corrections later, and it will be easier for you to see your errors.
- Don't correct grammar or edit sentences as you write. Just keep writing. Only edit during your last 10 or 15 minutes.

- Don't get stuck in the introduction. Keep moving forward. If you have extra time, you can always go back and add more information. If you're really stuck, write the body paragraphs first, leaving space to write an introduction later. Remember that introductions and conclusions can be a little shorter for timed essays than they are for essays that you write at home.
- Use clear, concise, even simple sentences. The more complex your sentences are, the more likely you are to make grammatical errors. Usually timed essays are graded more on content and organization than on style.
- If you do run out of time, write a note at the end saying "Did not finish, ran out of time." While this note may not save your grade, it may alert your instructor to the fact that you may have difficulty with timed essay exams (as opposed to the content of the exam or the course).

Proofreading / Editing the Essay

- Try to get some "distance" from the writing so that you will see the mistakes more clearly. Pretend that somebody else wrote it. Read the paragraphs out of order or from the last paragraph back to the first. Cover up the paper and read only one line at a time.
- If you know you don't have much time left, focus only on your most common error patterns.
- If you discover that you need to add information (like more concrete details or examples), write them into the margins or into the skipped lines. You can draw arrows to the added information if you need to.

PRACTICE

Use the strategies above, as well as the strategies for interpreting essay questions that you learned in Chapter 5, to help you answer one of these timed essay questions. If your instructor gives you 90 minutes for the test, follow this formula for time management:

15 minutes brainstorming / planning / outlining

60 minutes writing

15 minutes proofreading / editing

_____

90 minutes total

If you have only one hour, follow this formula:

10 minutes brainstorming / planning / outlining

40 minutes writing

10 minutes editing / proofreading

_____

60 minutes total

Topic choices:

1. Describe a job that you hope to have someday. Why do you want this job? What are the most important skills necessary for this job? What are the employment prospects in this field? What are you doing now to prepare yourself to get this job?

2. Describe a job that you held in the past. Was this job fulfilling or unfulfilling? (Did you like it or not?) Why? Explain your reasoning with specific examples.

3. Compare and/or contrast two jobs you have held in the past, or a past job with your current job. Describe the specific responsibilities of each one, or explain the process of doing your work at each job. Which job do you prefer? Why?

 **Orientation**

Finding Out about College Career Centers

Most colleges have a career center on campus. This is a place where students can find information about current job openings or companies that might be interested in hiring students or graduates from that college. Students may also be able to find information about internships, campus work-study jobs, summer jobs, job training sessions, and career fairs (events where companies come to recruit students or recent graduates). Some career centers may even offer help with writing resumes and cover letters, or offer practice job interviews ("mock interviews").

YOUR TASK

1. If you are currently in or near a college, find out if there is a career center on campus. If you are not currently in or near a college, use the Internet to research a college that interests you. Find out if their career center has a website. Or call the school directory and ask to be connected to the career center. You may be able to get recorded information or speak with someone who works in the center. Find answers to the following questions and write notes:

   Is there a career center?

   > If yes, where is it located?

   > If no, is there some other resource for job/career information on campus?

   When is the career center open?

   Who works in the career center? (Students? Trained job counselors?)

   How do you make an appointment? Is it possible to go there without one?

   What kinds of resources does the career center have? (What kinds of books? Is there computer/Internet access? Are there job directories? Other directories?)

Does the career center offer any special programs, training sessions, classes, or workshops? If so, what are they?

2. Compare your results with a small group or share them with the class. Did you find any information that surprised you? Would you be likely to use the career center? Why or why not?

▼ *Final Project*

Option 1: Give a Poster Presentation on a Career, a Company, or a College

Working alone, with a partner, or with a small group, prepare a formal oral presentation on a career that interests you, a company that interests you, or a college that interests you. (If you are working with a partner or a group, divide the presentation so that everyone speaks for the same amount of time.) Prepare a visual aid to go with your report. The visual can be on one or more posters. Your poster might show images, photographs, charts, graphs, or text. Use information, ideas, and vocabulary from this chapter as much as you can. Your presentation should answer the following question:

If you are presenting on a company:

- What is the company's name?
- Where is it located?
- How did you find out about this company?
- What is the company most well-known for? Does it produce something, or does it provide a service?
- How large is this company?
- What kinds of jobs are available in this company?
- Is this a good company to work for? Why or why not?

If you are presenting on a career choice:

- What is this career? What are some related careers?
- How do you prepare for this career? How much education do you need? What would you need to get a degree in, or major in? Do you need additional training?

- How much might one expect to earn in this career? (*Note:* Be careful if you are interviewing someone in this career; not everyone is comfortable stating what they make. It may be okay to ask about starting salary ranges.)
- Are their opportunities for advancement in this career? What are they? Would you like to pursue this career? Why or why not?

If you are presenting on a college:

- What is the college?
- Where is it located?
- How many people attend this college?
- What percentage of students are men? Women? People of different racial or ethnic backgrounds? International students?
- What kinds of degrees are offered at this college?
- What are some basic requirements for getting accepted into this college?
- How much is tuition?
- What kinds of facilities and resources do they have?
- What does the campus look like?
- Would you like to attend this college? Why or why not?

Option 2: Give a Poster Presentation on a Successful Individual

Working alone, with a partner or a small group, prepare a formal oral presentation on a person that you see as successful. Perhaps this person has achieved the American Dream, or perhaps this person has become successful in some other way. The person you choose can be a famous person that you research or someone you know personally. (If you are working with a partner or a group, divide the presentation so that everyone speaks for the same amount of time.) Prepare a visual aid to go with your report. The visual can be on one or more posters (large pieces of paper). Your poster might show images, photographs, charts, graphs, or text. Use information, ideas, and vocabulary from this chapter as much as you can.

Your presentation should answer the following questions:

- Who is this person? Where is he or she from? Is the person living or dead?
- If this is someone you know personally, how do you know this person? If this person is a famous person, what is he or she famous for?
- Did this person have a dream or a goal? If so, what was it? How did the person work toward achieving this dream or goal?
- Did this person face any obstacles? If so, what were they? How did this person overcome obstacles on the path to success?
- If you think this person has achieved "the American Dream," define the American Dream and explain how this person has achieved it. If you think that this person is successful for other reasons, explain what those are. Give specific examples and stories from the person's life.
- What do you most admire about this person?

▼ *Check Your Progress*

How are you doing so far? Put a check mark in the box that best explains how you feel about your progress in each category. Be sure to ask your instructor or classmates for help if there is something that you don't understand or that you would like to review.

Topic	I understand this topic very well; I feel confident about using it again.	I understand most of this topic; I feel moderately confident.	I understand some but not all of this topic.	I don't understand this topic well; I need to review.
Key Words				
Vocabulary Strategy 6: Using Synonyms to Define Words and Expand Vocabulary				
Speaking Strategy 6A: Giving a Formal Presentation				
Speaking Strategy 6B: Using Visual Aids in a Presentation				
Reading Strategy 6A: Identifying Word References				
Reading Strategy 6B: Making Inferences				
Listening Strategy 6: Organizing Notes into a Numeric Outline				
Writing Strategy 6A: Using Persuasive Language				
Writing Strategy 6B: Considering Opposing and Alternative Views				
Graphics Strategy 6: Creating Tables				
Test-Taking Strategy 6: Writing Timed Essays				
Orientation: Finding Out about Career Centers				

Which class participation tip(s) from Chapter 1 did you use?

_____

_____

Which small group participation job(s) did you do?

_____

_____

What was the most important thing you learned in this chapter?

_____

_____

If you checked "do not understand" for anything in the chart on page 196, write a question about that topic:

_____

_____

Look back at the personal learning goals you set in "Getting Started" on page xxvi. What did you do in this chapter to help yourself meet those goals?

_____

_____

Thinking of everything you have done so far in this book, do you think you have successfully met your original personal learning goals? Why or why not?

_____

_____

✍ **PART 2**

Writing Skills

In this section of the book, you can review or learn basic elements of academic writing. You can also learn some additional strategies for succeeding on college writing assignments. Pages in this section can be a reference for you as you complete the *Writing Strategies* and *Writing Tasks* in Chapters 1 through 6.

As you work through these two chapters, and as you work on your writing assignments, you may wish to keep a journal. A **journal** is a notebook, or a section of your notebook (or a computer file), where you can write freely and informally about a topic, exploring your ideas on the page. In a journal, you might write about your personal feelings and experiences related to a topic or a reading assignment. You might ask questions about a topic or a reading and try to answer them. Usually journals are not graded for grammar or spelling. Your professor may read them and make a few comments in them. Journals are a good place to get ideas for writing assignments; you can look back at your journal entries and see if there are ideas you can use or explore further. In addition, journals give you more practice with writing. The more you write, the easier writing will become for you.

Some journal topics are suggested throughout Chapters 7 and 8 to encourage you to think about how you can improve your writing. Your professor may suggest additional journal topics related to the themes and readings in Chapters 1 through 6.

Sample Student Journal

Journal #1   Reaction to the article "Intercultural Stumbling Blocks"

This article made me think a lot about how difficult it is to adjust to a new culture. I could really relate to some of the ideas in the article, especially about language and speaking in class. For example, I have a hard time when I have to give an opinion during our class discussions. Sometimes, I feel that Americans are over-confident and they barely accept the others' opinions. To illustrate the point, during our last chemistry class discussion, American students in my group just worked on the assigned problem to get the correct result, and they didn't discuss anything with each other. However, I was the only person in the group who could find the correct result. Finally, they accepted my result, but it took time. They did not accept my result until they had finished trying to do the problem themselves. I wondered if this was because I am an international student, but I think Americans don't want to rely on others. In my country, most of the students discuss each other's opinions and ideas openly and enthusiastically. They warmly appreciate each other's ideas, even if they don't agree. The article "Intercultural Stumbling Blocks" made me think about this experience. I wonder if I experienced a real cultural difference, or if it is just this group of people. I have other classes where people do seem to enjoy sharing ideas and are open to listening to my ideas. Maybe, then, this article is too general. Maybe it needed to consider other possibilities and look at more examples. I will bring up this point in our next class discussion.

7 ～ Writing Paragraphs and Essays

The Writing Process

The process of writing involves three main steps: planning, drafting, and revising. In the **planning** stage, you read the topic or assignment carefully, generate ideas (by brainstorming, listing, clustering, or freewriting), choose the best ideas to use, and outline your ideas. In the **drafting** stage, you use your notes and outline to write the assignment. (A **draft** is a first or early version of a writing assignment.) It does not need to be perfect at this stage. It is an attempt to make your notes and outline look more like a real paragraph or essay. Your writing assignment may go through more than one draft. In the **revising** stage, you review and rewrite the assignment. Most people revise more than once. You might revise an assignment one or more times to make the ideas more clear; to make sure you are following the assignment guidelines; to add or subtract information; to make the sentences more varied and interesting; or to correct grammatical, spelling, and typing errors. A professor may also ask you to revise (or give you an option to revise); for this type of revising, you would probably incorporate **feedback** (comments and suggestions) from the professor.

Journal

1. What part of the writing process is easiest for you? Why? What part is the most difficult? Why?

2. What are your strengths as a writer? What do you think you need to work on most in your writing?

3. Do you like to write (either in English or in your native language)? Why or why not? If you do like to write, what kinds of writing do you enjoy? (Creative writing? Lab reports? Essays? Something else?)

Formatting Your Writing Assignments

All of your written work in college should have a professional appearance. College professors will almost never accept handwritten work for formal assignments, work with a large computer font (14 point or higher), or work with margins that are too wide or too small. You should also staple or paper clip your pages together and put your name on every page. An example of a standard format for the first page of a paper, with some additional guidelines, is provided.

Journal

1. Look back at a previous writing assignment, perhaps one you have done for another class in the past. Is it formatted correctly? Does it meet all the guidelines? Would a professor accept it for a class? Why or why not?

2. How important do you think the appearance of college papers is? Why do you think college professors care so much about the format? (Aren't they interested in your ideas too?) In your experience, was format important for high school papers as well? If you have lived and gone to school in another country, did you use this format or a different one? Was the appearance of your written work important there too?

[Your name]

[Your professor's name]

[Name of the course / section]

[Date]

[Sample Paper Format:]

Center the Title and Subtitles

This is an example of a basic format for a college paper. Always indent the first line of each paragraph. Press the "Tab" key on the computer once.

Do not leave extra spaces between paragraphs. Double space the entire document. Use standard margins: one inch on the left, right, top, and bottom. This leaves room for the professor to write any comments.

Use a 12-point computer font. If you use larger fonts (14-point or more), you are not writing as much as everyone else, and the professor may think you are trying to write less than the assignment requires. If you use smaller fonts (10-point or smaller), you are writing more than the assignment requires, and your paper will be harder to read. Use traditional, standard fonts like Times New Roman (which this document uses), Courier, Arial, Palatino, or Geneva. Don't use unusual or artistic fonts; they are hard to read and distract the reader from the content of your paper.

Number your pages if you have more than one. Put your last name on the top of every page, next to the page number. Don't put your paper in a special report cover or use special bindings, unless you are asked to. Always clip or staple your pages together.

Paragraph Structure, Unity, Development, and Coherence

Paragraphs for academic papers usually have three parts: a main idea, supporting points and details, and a concluding statement. In addition, **unity** (the paragraph is focused on only one topic), **development** (the paragraph is of a sufficient length), and **coherence** (the sentences and ideas "flow" smoothly, or fit together clearly) are all parts of good paragraph writing.

STRUCTURE

Paragraphs usually have three main parts: **a topic sentence, supporting points or details,** and **a concluding statement.**

1. The Topic Sentence

The main idea of a paragraph is usually stated in a topic sentence. The **topic sentence** is usually the first sentence, but it may also appear at the end of the paragraph or in the middle. Occasionally, the topic sentence is not directly stated; it is implied, meaning we can understand what the main idea is by looking at the information or examples in the paragraph. Here is an example of a paragraph where the topic sentence is implied. What do all of the ideas and example have in common? Do you see a word or phrase that repeats in the paragraph? Based on these ideas and examples, what do you think a good topic sentence would be for this paragraph?

> One solution to the parking problem on our campus would be to hold a lottery for available parking spaces. The lottery would be held just before the start of each semester. Students who received a space in a lot for one semester would be ineligible for a space in the following semester. This would give more students a chance of winning a space. However, many students would probably complain that this system is unfair. Therefore, another possible solution might be to award parking spaces based on seniority. Fourth-year and third-year students would have priority over second-year and first-year students. The problem with this solution, however, is that many first-year students don't know the area or the campus well; they may not know where else to park. They may also feel unwelcome at their new school if they are told that they cannot park there. The best solution, then, might be to take over the visitors' parking lot or to limit the number of visitors' spaces. These are often empty spaces anyway, ex-

cept during Orientation Week and campus events. These spaces should be given to paying students until a new parking lot can be built.

All of these ideas and examples are about *solutions to the campus parking problem*. (Notice that these words repeat in the paragraph.) A possible topic sentence would be as follows: *There are several possible solutions to the campus parking problem, but there are problems with these solutions.*

A topic sentence usually has two parts: a main topic and an idea about that topic. The idea is usually an opinion about or an aspect of that topic. This part of the topic sentence gives a more specific focus to the paragraph. For example, here are two topic sentences for a paragraph about a college:

    main topic   **specific idea: an aspect of the topic**

Wentworth Institute of Technology <u>offers many engineering technology majors</u>.

    main topic   **specific idea: an opinion about the topic**

Wentworth Institute of Technology <u>has a strong electromechanical engineering program</u>.

A main topic might have many different possible specific ideas. In the examples above, the main topic is the same. There are at least two possible specific ideas that could be developed into a paragraph.

Journal

Write as many topic sentences as you can about the school you are attending now or a school you attended in the past. The main idea of your topic sentence is the name of the school. The specific idea of your topic sentences will be aspects of or opinions about the school.

2. SUPPORTING DETAILS

Topic sentences must be supported with specific details and examples. Remember, the reader may not always agree with or understand your topic sentence. You must prove your point with enough information so that the reader will see your point. Some types of details you can give are as follows.

- **Descriptive Details.** Describe something so that the reader can see it or feel it. Use details related to the senses: sight, sound, smell, taste, or touch.

- **Facts.** These could include information from other sources (research), information that you know to be true, statistics, or other data.
- **Anecdotes.** Anecdotes are brief stories. You could tell a story from your own experience or your observations or knowledge of somebody else.
- **Quotations from Experts.** If you use somebody else's words to prove or explain your point, remember to use quotation marks around them (" ") and don't change their words.

3. CONCLUDING STATEMENTS

Avoid ending a paragraph with examples. Always try to add at least one sentence (you may need more) to make your point clear. You can explain or comment on the examples, return to the idea in your topic sentence, or make a transition into the next paragraph.

PRACTICE

Read the following examples of paragraphs written by students. Underline the topic sentence in each paragraph. Label the main topic (M) and the specific idea (S). Highlight, or list on a separate page, the specific examples that you see. What kinds of examples are they? Finally, draw a circle around the concluding statement(s) or highlight it in a different color.

Example 1

Ever since I was a little girl, the backyard of my house in the Dominican Republic has been my favorite place to be because it is so peaceful. Even when I am writing this paragraph, I can see the trees being moved by the soft wind, which reminds me of the beginning of a ritual. The blue sky looks like a big cotton blanket. The garden is filled with all kinds of trees: cherry, mango, beans, and avocado trees. Colorful birds fly from tree to tree, singing sweet melodies. I can remember how those birds used to wake me up, inspiring me to write and to dream. In the backyard of my old house, even in my mind, I am part of nature, peaceful and free. There I am nothing more than a soul.

Example 2

Almost all Americans are work-oriented. In their conversations, the most important theme is "work." As an example, I used to work in an insurance company, and at lunchtime, when you are supposed to relax, all my co-workers did was talk about their jobs. I couldn't believe my ears. In my culture, when people are eating they talk about other things, never about work. I think this constant talking about work is one reason why people hate their jobs at some point. As another example, one of the associates in the insurance company told me that she had a second job at nights, and that she worked so hard because she had a child to support. She was always feeling stressed, and she got sick a lot. I don't think this amount of working is healthy for the mind or the body. Finally, I can add my own example of something that happened while I worked in this company. After just a few months of working there, I could not quit. Even when I started college, I kept working part-time, and I still work. I got used to working—or, more importantly, I got used to the money. The work-oriented American culture can change anybody. It is like a virus. Once it gets into you, it is hard to get out. Unfortunately, I think that you can lose a lot with this attitude. You can put all your energy into work and forget about your family.

Example 3

Japanese people are very formal in the way they talk to other people, especially to elder people. Unlike in the United States, Japanese people show their respect in their way of speaking. There are three different ways of speaking depending on who you are talking to. One involves using "courtesy words." Courtesy words are used when you talk to acquaintances or strangers. There are also "honorific words." These are used when you are talking to any kind of elder person, such as a teacher. Finally, there are "modest words." These words have tricky rules that even a lot of Japanese people have to be careful with because they seem similar to honorific words. However, there is a significant difference between honorific words and modest words. Honorific words show respect towards the person to whom you are speaking, but modest words show humility. This type of speaking is used when you are working. For instance, you might use modest words when you are calling another company or answering calls from other companies. These differences of words can be hard even for Japanese people because we never study them in school. However, understanding these word differences is one of the most important skills to have when interviewing for a job.

Example 4

The United States and Korea have many differences in teaching styles. Education in America tends to be more liberal and creative. Students do a lot of experiments and presentations. They learn how to solve problems themselves. In addition, they are taught to express their opinion in speeches and in writing. Moreover, students work frequently in groups to learn leadership and cooperation skills. Finally, parents and teachers don't physically punish or discipline children. In contrast, Korean parents and teachers tend to educate students to get good scores on exams. Students must memorize formulas and information from books. They do not do many creative projects or work in groups. Koreans think that punishment is necessary to discipline children, and physical punishments are permitted in schools. The Korean system of education may be changing, however. More recently, Koreans have been trying to change their teaching style and educate children more liberally and creatively.

Journal

1. Which of the example paragraphs do you like best? Why? What strategies does the writer use that appeal to you? Which of the example paragraphs do you like least? Why? If you think any of these could be improved, how would you improve them? Could other types of details or examples be added to them? What types?

2. What type of writing assignment do you think each of the example paragraphs might have been written for? Do you think that any of these paragraphs could be part of a longer essay? If so, what do you think might come in the paragraphs before or after them?

PARAGRAPH UNITY

Unity means one. A paragraph has unity when it is focused on only one idea. If other ideas come into the paragraph, we say the paragraph is not *unified*. Always look back at the topic sentence. Do all the sentences that follow relate to it or support it? If not, cut or move sentences or examples that do not relate.

PRACTICE

The following paragraph lacks unity. Underline or highlight the sentences that do not directly relate to the topic sentence.

The cafeteria at our school needs improvement in many ways. First of all, it needs to offer a wider variety of foods. Most students purchase the meal plan, which means that they must eat two or three meals in the cafeteria every day. The way the meal plan works is that students use their identification card to pay for their food, and pre-paid meal "points" are automatically deducted from the card for each meal. Many students complain that there are not enough choices and that they are tired of eating the same foods every day. Some of these students eventually may stop eating in the cafeteria, and spend their money on snack food or junk food, which is not healthy. There are not many good, affordable restaurants in the area, and this is another big problem. It would be really great if a food court moved in to the area so that students didn't have to use the cafeteria at all. More importantly, however, there is research suggesting that it is not healthy to eat the same food every day. We need variety in our diet in order to stay healthy. Secondly, the cafeteria needs to serve healthier foods.

A lot of the foods they serve are very greasy. Moreover, the cafeteria serves a lot of pizza, hamburgers, and fried foods. Students who are away from home for the first time do not always know how to eat right. They may not understand how eating a balanced diet can improve their ability to do well in school. The health center should offer educational workshops on healthy eating. Finally, the cafeteria should be redesigned to make it a more comfortable and attractive place for students to meet and socialize. Right now, there are not enough tables, and the tables are too close together. It is an uncomfortable and unpleasant environment. Students eat quickly and leave. People might enjoy their food more, and slow down when they eat, if the cafeteria were more attractive. Some researchers are concerned that Americans eat too quickly, and this can negatively affect our digestion of food. These three improvements to the cafeteria might be a little bit expensive, but they are an important investment in the health of the student body.

PARAGRAPH DEVELOPMENT

How long should a paragraph be? You may see paragraphs of only one or two sentences in newspapers, magazines, and fiction. However, in academic writing, this is usually considered too short. You might get a comment saying "paragraph is undeveloped" if you write paragraphs that are this short. **Paragraph development** is adding enough details and examples to support the point in your topic sentence.

Some people say that five sentences is a good rule. This gives you one sentence for the topic sentence, three sentences for details and examples, and one concluding sentence. This model can be useful if you are trying to find ideas or plan a paragraph. However, it is not a good rule for every paragraph. Paragraph length may depend on the topic of your paragraph. For some points, you may need many examples—and different types of examples—to use as support. For other points, you may be able to use just one or two very strong examples. Sometimes you might use an example that needs explanation. (This is especially true when you're using quotations—you may need to explain somebody else's words in your own words, or to simplify the language in the quote.) Therefore, do not restrict yourself to having only five sentences in a paragraph.

Can a paragraph ever be too long? Yes. If a paragraph is approaching one page, or if it goes on for more than one page, it is usually a sign that the paragraph is unfocused—that it is about more than one thing. It is also usually too much for the reader to process at once. Paragraph breaks help the reader to pause and take in the information before going on to the next point. Therefore, if your paragraphs are too long, look back at them for places where you could break into one or more new paragraphs. Specifically, look for changes in time (time words like *first, later, in the next century, ten years later, the following months*, etc., can signal significant time shifts). Other places you might use for paragraph breaks are steps in a process, shifts in thought, reasons for an opinion, causes/effects, and comparisons/contrasts (moving from one thing to the next thing that is being compared or contrasted).

PRACTICE

1. The following paragraphs are *undeveloped*. The first one is not long enough, and there are not enough examples to support the topic sentence. The second one looks long enough, but the sentences are not specific enough to support the topic sentence; the whole paragraph feels too general. How could each one be developed? Make a mark like this— ∧ —to show where you could add examples or details. What types of examples or details could be added? On separate sheets of paper, rewrite each paragraph.

Paragraph A

Americans suffer from the problem of overwork. They don't take enough vacations. They work long hours. Compared with people in other countries, Americans work too much.

Paragraph B

Americans value equality. It is true that the United States still has many example of inequality, like some poor people don't have rights. However, Americans still value the idea of equality in society, and they actively work toward this goal. The government and some volunteer organizations try to help them fix problems of equality, which shows how Americans are interested in trying to solve problems of inequality and make society better.

2. The following paragraph is *overdeveloped:* it is too long and loses its focus. Look for one or more places to start a new paragraph. Rewrite it, adding new topic sentences if necessary. If any of the new paragraphs look undeveloped, add examples or details.

First-year college students should try to live on campus, with a roommate, if it is at all possible. There are significant reasons why this choice will benefit them personally and academically. First, they will have more opportunities to make friends if they live on campus. They might be able to find a study group more easily, and most people would agree that studying with a group is more beneficial than studying individually. Furthermore, they can learn new study skills from their roommates or other people in the dorms. Many people use different tricks for studying the material outside of class, and if you don't live on campus, you might not get these ideas. To illustrate my point, I personally learned how to read schedules and manage my study times from observing one of my roommates who used a good system. In addition, there are more people on campus who can offer emotional support during difficult times. If students live alone off-campus, they might feel too isolated. They could even become depressed. Finally, it is good for students to meet people from all different backgrounds, talk about many different subjects, and be exposed to different points of view. This is good preparation for the real world, where you must deal with all kinds of people. It is especially important for international students to try to live on campus. Living on campus can help international students to adjust to American college life more quickly. They will learn different cultural customs more quickly. They will also improve their English more quickly than they would if they lived off campus with people who speak the same language, such as their family. International students can easily feel isolated, and living on campus provides many opportunities for them to connect with others.

EXTRA PRACTICE

Write a new, well-developed paragraph on the same topic as the main idea of one of the paragraphs above. However, take the *opposite* position and choose new details and examples to support that opinion.

PARAGRAPH COHERENCE

When the ideas "flow" or "fit together" smoothly, we say that a paragraph has **coherence.** To *cohere* means to come together. We can use many different signal words to connect ideas and therefore improve coherence. These signal words can connect sentences within a paragraph; they can also connect paragraphs together, when they are used as transitions in topic sentences. However, keep in mind that if a paragraph does not have unity or development, or if the content of the sentences is not clear, these signal words alone do not create coherence. They help to highlight, or make more obvious, the connections between the ideas that are already there. These words are not substitutes for careful thinking and writing.

Signal Words and Phrases	Purpose
First, Secondly, Thirdly, Next, In addition, Additionally, Also, Besides that, Furthermore, Moreover	Ordering information, adding information (especially adding similar information)
First, Second, Next, After that, Afterward, Then, Meanwhile, Subsequently, In the end	Listing ideas in time order (chronological sequence)
But, However, Nevertheless, Nonetheless, In contrast, On the other hand, Alternatively, Conversely	Showing contrasting information or ideas
Similarly, Likewise, Along those lines, In comparison	Showing similarities
For instance, For example, To illustrate, Specifically, As an example, An example of that is . . .	Showing an example
In other words, That is, That is to say, What I mean by that is . . .	Clarifying and explaining
Indeed, In fact, As a matter of fact, Interestingly, Significantly	Adding emphasis
As a result, Consequently, Thus, Therefore	Showing results or conclusions

PRACTICE

Reread the example paragraphs given for unity and development on the previous pages. Circle any signal words you see that give the paragraph coherence. Note the function of each signal word (to show additional information, to show contrast, etc.).

Journal

Look back at some of your past writing assignments. What do you think your paragraphs most need work on? Structure, unity, development, or coherence? Choose one paragraph from a past writing assignment and critique it. What paragraph elements are you using? What ones do you need to use or improve?

Essay Structure

An academic essay has three main parts: the **introduction,** the **body,** and the **conclusion.** Typically, the body of an essay has three or more paragraphs. A standard length for a short (two- to three-page) essay is a five-paragraph essay. This is also a good length of an essay for a timed writing situation. However, some essays may require more than five paragraphs. For example, if you were assigned a five- to six-page essay, you would need more than five paragraphs or your five paragraphs would be much too long. Also, even with a short essay, you may find that you have a lot to say in one or two paragraphs, and that they need to be broken up into smaller ones. Don't rely on the five-paragraph formula all the time. It is just a guideline to help you remember the structure of a good essay. Just like your paragraphs, the *content* of your essay may determine the form. For most of the writing tasks in this book, however, and in your first year of college, thinking in terms of a five-paragraph essay is a good place to start.

INTRODUCTION AND THESIS STATEMENT

The **introduction** of an essay should introduce the topic; it might also try to get the reader interested in the topic. You could start with questions, an interesting quotation, a surprising fact, a controversial issue, a summary of a text, a definition of a key word, or a short anecdote. You can also start with general ideas about a topic and then, with each sentence, focus more on the main idea of the essay, ending the introduction paragraph with a thesis statement.

Just as a topic sentence is a controlling idea for a paragraph, a **thesis statement** is a controlling idea for an entire essay. A good thesis will state a clear opinion, or argument, about the topic. It may also predict the organization of the essay. It almost always appears as the last sentence of the introduction, not the first. Each body paragraph should clearly support the thesis.

A thesis statement should state an opinion. You should be able to imagine people disagreeing with you. Words like *should, should not, must, have to* can clearly signal opinions. However, for some topics those words don't seem to work well. For example, if you are writing a paper about a text, giving your opinion about an article or a book, you probably would not use those words. Therefore, you have to imagine people disagreeing with you. Are you stating something obvious, or could people have a different opinion? You may also be able to use opinion-signalling words like *most important, most significantly, better, worse, more effectively, less effectively*.

A thesis statement can predict the essay's organization by briefly mentioning key words that will appear in the topic sentences of the body paragraphs. This gives the reader a kind of "map" of the essay—it is clear where it is going—and it helps keep you, the writer, focused.

Finally, a good thesis is not too general and not too specific. If you cannot find at least three supporting points for it, or if those supporting points cannot each be developed with examples, perhaps the thesis is really a more focused topic sentence for a paragraph.

PRACTICE

1. Here are some examples of possible thesis statements. Discuss in a small group, or in your journal, why two are good thesis statements and two are not.

   Thesis about an issue: The school library should update its computers, purchase more books and journals, and extend its hours on weekends.

   Not a thesis: The school library has 10,000 books in its collection.

   Not a thesis: The school library is open from 8:00 to 4:30 on weekends.

   Thesis about a text: In Gish Jen's novel *Typical American,* the family of Chinese-Americans are held together by their economic situation, their love for each other, and, most importantly, by their cultural values.

   Not a thesis: The novel *Typical American* was written by Gish Jen, a Chinese-American writer.

2. Here is an example introduction from a student essay. Underline the thesis statement. Then predict: What will the rest of the essay be about? Can you tell from the thesis what the writer will discuss in the three body paragraphs that follow? How can you tell?

> What is the definition of the American Dream? People may have slightly different ideas about this concept. Basically, it is the desire to improve your life or your circumstances, to become successful by having a good job or a house and a family. I would like to define this concept a little differently. In my view, the American Dream has two forms: the community American Dream and the individual American Dream. The first one is what an entire community—or even the whole country—desires. The second one is the personal hopes of individual Americans. The novel *Typical American*, by Gish Jen, focuses more on the idea of the individual American dream. In this novel about a Chinese immigrant family, we see different versions of the American Dream. Three characters—Ralph Chang, his sister Theresa, and the "self-made man" Grover, each have slightly different ideas of the American Dream and different personal goals.

3. Which would be the best **thesis statement** for a **five-paragraph essay**? Why?

   a. Technology is advancing by leaps and bounds.
   b. Throughout the twentieth century, the United States witnessed many important technological advances.
   c. One technological innovation intended to help people manage time is the Palm Pilot.
   d. Advances in electronics products may be exciting; however, technology has also made products high in cost, complicated to operate, and inferior in craftsmanship.

BODY

The **body** of an essay usually has at least three well-developed paragraphs. Each paragraph should clearly relate to the thesis. The topic sentence of each paragraph can repeat key words (or synonyms of key words) that are used in the thesis statement.

Think carefully about the order of the body paragraphs. It's usually best to lead up to your most important point. That way the essay will seem to be "moving," or "building," toward the final point. Sometimes we don't always know the best order of the body paragraphs until we have written a first draft. Look carefully at your draft. Do you have a lot to say about one topic sentence compared with another? Is one of your paragraphs thinner, or less developed, than another? Often the more developed paragraphs are more important and should appear near the end.

PRACTICE

Choose one of the topics of any of the example paragraphs earlier in this chapter. Write an outline for an essay of five or more paragraphs. Think of topics you could use for each body paragraph. Then incorporate key words from those topics into a thesis statement.

CONCLUSION

Conclusions can be hard to write. You may feel as though you have already said everything important. Nevertheless, it is important to give the essay a sense of closure. You can conclude an essay by restating your thesis statement in a new way and by summarizing your main points. However, you should try to do something more than that. Make it clear to your readers why they should care about this topic, or why they should see your point of view. Think about larger questions and issues. Try some of these strategies.

- Look back at your introduction. See if you can return to it in some way. If you started with a quote, go back to that quote; now that we've read the essay, do we understand the quote more? If you asked questions in the introduction, can you answer them in the conclusion? If you started with an anecdote, can you return to that anecdote in some way? If you started with a definition, has your essay shown how this definition is more complex than it might first appear?

- If your essay is mostly about your personal experience, try to expand the topic—make it more general—in the conclusion. How can other readers relate to it? Does your experience teach us all something?

- If your essay is focused on an issue or a text, try to use your personal experience or reactions in the conclusion.

PRACTICE

1. Here is an example of a conclusion from a student essay. What strategies is the writer using to conclude? Discuss the strategies with a partner or a group, or write about them in your journal.

> In conclusion, the three characters' different hopes and dreams complicate our idea of the American Dream in the novel *Typical American*. Ralph's American Dream is to become successful as a professional and to provide for his family. Theresa's American Dream is to find love and happiness. Grover's American Dream is to get rich—even if he has to break the law to do so. There is not just one idea of an American Dream, but many, and they can vary from person to person. However, the whole concept of the American Dream itself—a communal desire to be successful—is uniquely American. I would argue that the Changs fell into a trap when they started pursuing their dreams at the expense of their family relationships. The opportunities and freedom that America offered made them "Typical Americans." They forgot their identity as Chinese. Because of this message, I think this is an important novel not only for immigrants but also for Americans. Jen describes clearly how living in America is not a fairy tale story. It is hard to live here and to hold on to your identity in the face of new goals and opportunities. This story made me see a different view of America. There is a positive and a negative side to this country and to the American Dream. However, the novel also makes me think that we could have some control over how we pursue our American Dreams, and the experiences of these three characters in particular show us how.

2. Look back at the essay you outlined in the previous activity. How would you write a conclusion for it? Discuss your ideas with a partner or a group, or write your ideas in your journal.

Journal

1. If you have gone to school in another country, compare the style and structure of academic essays that you wrote there with the style and structure of American academic essays. Are they similar? Different? In what ways?

2. If you have written essays in English before, which part of the essay is the hardest for you to write: the introduction, thesis statement, body paragraphs, or conclusion? Why? Which part is the easiest? Why?

8 ～ Study Skills for Writing

In this chapter, you will learn some more specific strategies for succeeding on written assignments and improving your writing.

Keeping a Grammar/Error Log

Having a high number of grammar mistakes can negatively affect your grade on a writing assignment. Some professors may not even accept papers with a high number of grammatical errors. They may require you to rewrite the paper or to seek help with your writing from a tutor or some other resource. Therefore, although a few mistakes now and then are permissible, it's important to do everything you can on your own to improve your grammar. Find a tutor, take a review class, or review grammatical rules in a textbook.

Another thing you can do to improve your grammar is to keep a **log,** or list, of the types of grammatical errors you make in your writing. It can be frustrating to get a paper back from a professor and see many errors marked. On the other hand, you can view these marks as useful information that you can learn from. Write the errors, error types, and corrections in your log each time a writing assignment is returned to you. Notice the patterns of errors you make. Review these error types in a book or with a tutor. Before you hand in the next assignment, review your grammar log. Check your paper for the types of errors you have listed. Over time, you should see the amount of errors decrease.

Like a vocabulary log, a grammar log can be handwritten and in a section of your notebook, or it can be typed on the computer. Here is a sample grammar log:

Sentence with Error	Error Type (or Reason for Error)	Correction
<u>Everybody</u> <u>have to</u> carry the things <u>they needs</u>.	Subject-verb agreement (plural subject needs plural verb)	<u>Everybody</u> <u>has to</u> carry the things <u>they need</u>.
I came <u>to United States</u> in 1999.	Article ("United States" needs definite article the)	I came <u>to the United States</u> in 1999.
Americans feel they are <u>in-dividualism, privacy</u>, and <u>self-reliance</u>.	Word form errors (need adjectives after "be" verb, not nouns—or need to change the verb to go with nouns)	Americans feel they are <u>in-dividualistic, private</u>, and <u>self-reliant</u>. OR: Americans <u>value</u> individualism, privacy, and self-reliance.

PRACTICE

Look back at a recent writing assignment that an instructor has written comments on. Find three to five errors that you think are important. (Do you have more than one of this type of error? Is this a grammar error that you have not noticed before, or is it from a sentence that you thought was correct?) Start a grammar log.

Journal

1. What kinds of grammar errors do you usually make in your writing? Why do you think you continue to make these errors? (For example, is it because your language is very different from English? Is it because of the way you were taught grammar or writing? Is it because of your own level of effort?) What can you do to help eliminate these errors?

2. Find an example of writing that you like—a short paragraph or a few sentences. You could find this from a magazine, a work of fiction, a website, or from a reading in this book. Copy the section that you like in your journal. Then discuss what you like about it. Do you like the choice of words? Look closely at the sentences: are they long or short? Varied? Are there grammatical structures that you recognize? After you analyze the writing, try to write a paragraph on a different topic, imitating the style as much as possible.

222 STRATEGIES FOR COLLEGE SUCCESS

Understanding Your Professors' Comments

Pay close attention to the written feedback you receive on your writing assignments; this can help you to improve your writing on a revision of the assignment or on future assignments. If you ever have trouble understanding a professor's handwriting or comments, be sure to ask for clarification. Professors usually respond to your writing in three ways.

- **Marginal comments** are brief comments written in the margins of the paper. The professor may react to things you are saying with phrases like *yes!* or *good point*. If the professor does not understand what you are trying to say, he or she may write a question mark, write *unclear*, or ask questions that are intended to help you clarify your idea. If you have a chance to revise a paper, you should always make changes or clarifications based on marginal comments. Read marginal comments carefully. Sometimes a correction is not necessary; a professor may just write additional ideas related to yours as a way of making you think more about the topic, but it may not be necessary to change or add anything.

- **End comments** are notes at the end of the paper, usually next to your grade. These comments may be one or several sentences; they could also be a paragraph or more. They may contain information about what is well-done in your paper, questions your paper raises, and things you could do for improvement. If you have a chance to revise the paper, you should consider these end comments in your revision. If you may not revise the paper, you should review the end comments before your write your next paper. That way, you can avoid repeating errors, and keep doing things that worked well.

- **Sentence corrections** are brief notes indicating grammatical, spelling, or typing errors. Sometimes errors are circled with no explanation; sometimes the professor will use an abbreviation or symbol (listed on the next page) to tell you what type of error you have made. Usually a professor will not circle or identify every error in a paper. If you have a chance to revise an assignment, you are responsible for going through the paper carefully and looking for the types of errors that the professor identified. The professor is not your editor.

Here is a list of abbreviations and symbols your professor may use. A grammar handbook will give more information on them and explain how to correct them.

Sentence Correction Symbol or Note	Meaning
Awk	Awkward (problem with a phrase or a sentence structure; does not read smoothly)
Frag	Sentence fragment; incomplete sentence (the sentence is a phrase or a dependent clause by itself, so it can't stand alone as a sentence)
cap; ≡	Need to use a capital letter
LC	Need to use a lower-case letter, not capital
s-v agreement **s-v** **agr**	Subject-verb agreement error (the subject of the sentence may be singular but you're using a plural verb form, or the subject may be plural but you're using a singular verb form)
WW	Wrong word (word choice error; check your dictionary)
WF	Word form error (you may be using a noun where you need an adjective or a verb; you may be using an adverb instead of an adjective)
Prep	Preposition error (missing or incorrect preposition)
CS	Comma splice (incorrect comma use: you are using a comma between two independent clauses)
r-o; run-on	Run-on sentence (the sentence is too long and does not use correct punctuation)
VF	Verb form error (incomplete or incorrect form of a verb phrase)
VT	Verb tense error (wrong tense)
Sp	Spelling error
⌣	Reverse the order of words or phrases
¶	Need a new paragraph here

PRACTICE

Look back at a past writing assignment with written feedback from an instructor. What form of feedback is mostly used? Do you see any sentence corrections listed in the chart? Are there any comments you do not understand? How could you ask for clarification? Share your feedback with a partner or a group, or write about it in a journal.

Journal

1. What do you think professors should comment on more: your ideas, your grammar, or both equally? Are grammar, content, and organization all equally important in your opinion? Why or why not?

2. Have you ever received a grade on a writing assignment that you did not think was fair? What happened? What did you do? Would you handle the situation differently now? What would you do if you did not agree with a college professor's grade on a writing assignment?

Proofreading and Editing Tips

Before you turn in a writing assignment, you should always proofread carefully for errors. Proofreading is a type of revising that you do right before you are ready to hand something in. You should proofread only after you are satisfied with the content and organization of the essay. (You don't want to spend time correcting sentences that you may end up deleting.)

PRACTICE

Choose one of the strategies listed in the Tip Box and proofread a writing assignment that you are about to hand in or a copy of a previous writing assignment with no written feedback on it.

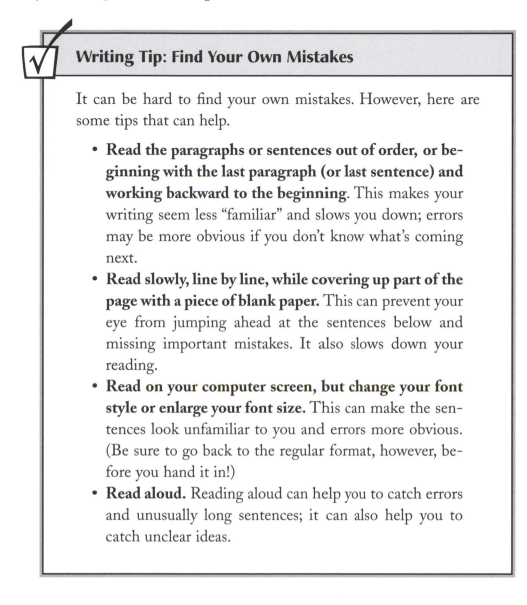

Writing Tip: Find Your Own Mistakes

It can be hard to find your own mistakes. However, here are some tips that can help.

- **Read the paragraphs or sentences out of order, or beginning with the last paragraph (or last sentence) and working backward to the beginning.** This makes your writing seem less "familiar" and slows you down; errors may be more obvious if you don't know what's coming next.
- **Read slowly, line by line, while covering up part of the page with a piece of blank paper.** This can prevent your eye from jumping ahead at the sentences below and missing important mistakes. It also slows down your reading.
- **Read on your computer screen, but change your font style or enlarge your font size.** This can make the sentences look unfamiliar to you and errors more obvious. (Be sure to go back to the regular format, however, before you hand it in!)
- **Read aloud.** Reading aloud can help you to catch errors and unusually long sentences; it can also help you to catch unclear ideas.

Basic Peer Review or Self-Review Checklists

Your instructor in this class may ask you at some point to do a **peer review**—in other words, to share a draft of a writing assignment with a partner or a small group and to give each other feedback. Your instructor may give you a list of specific things to look for. If you are not given a list, however, or if you do a peer review outside of class, you can use the following basic list of points to check for. (You can also use these for self-review; try pretending that you are reading a paper written by somebody else.)

Writing Tip: Basic Checklist for a Paragraph

- ❑ Is there a topic sentence? (Underline it or write it on a separate piece of paper.)
- ❑ Does the topic sentence have a main idea? (If so, label it M.)
- ❑ Does the topic sentence have a specific idea? (If so, label it S.)
- ❑ Is the paragraph developed with supporting details or examples? (If so, highlight them, or list them on a separate piece of paper.) What kinds of details or examples are they? Are there enough of them? Too many? Is the paragraph too long or too short?
- ❑ Does the paragraph have a least one concluding statement? (If so, circle it, or write it on a separate piece of paper.)
- ❑ Does the paragraph have unity? Do all the details and examples clearly relate to the topic sentence? (If not, put an X by details or sentences that do not seem to relate.)
- ❑ Does the paragraph have coherence? Circle any signal words that you can find. Are there enough of them? Do they express the correct relationship between ideas?
- ❑ Does your writing assignment have the correct format (margins, typed, double-spaced, your name)?

Writing Tip: Check Your Essay

❑ Does the essay clearly have an introduction, a body, and a conclusion (a beginning, middle, and end)?

❑ Does the introduction introduce the main idea in an interesting way?

❑ Does the introduction end with a thesis statement? (If you can find a thesis or possible thesis, highlight it or write it on a separate piece of paper.)

❑ Does the thesis state an opinion? (If you think it does, label it Opinion.)

❑ Does the thesis predict the essay's organization, perhaps by briefly listing supporting points? (If so, label the supporting points a, b, c, or write them on a separate piece of paper.)

❑ Does each body paragraph have a topic sentence? (If so, highlight them or write them on a separate piece of paper.)

❑ Does each topic sentence have a main idea and a specific idea? If so, label them M and S.

❑ Does each paragraph have a clear structure: topic sentence, details, and concluding statement? (If not, put an X by any paragraph that does not have a clear or complete structure.)

❑ Does each paragraph have unity?

❑ Does each paragraph have adequate development?

❑ Does each paragraph have coherence? (Circle signal words that you see. Are there enough of them? Do they express the correct relationship between ideas?)

❑ Does the essay have a conclusion? Does the conclusion restate the main points and do something else to show the larger point of the essay? Should anything be added to the conclusion?

❑ Does your writing assignment have the correct format (margins, typed, double-spaced, your name)?

APPENDIX A

Vocabulary Log

New Word	Sentence you found or heard it in	Word form (noun, verb, adjective, adverb)	Other word forms it can take	Definition	Use the word in your own sentence

Blank Schedule

	Monday	Tuesday	Wednesday	Thursday	Friday	Saturday	Sunday
7:00–8:00							
8:00–9:00							
9:00–10:00							
10:00–11:00							
11:00–12:00							
12:00–1:00							
1:00–2:00							
2:00–3:00							
3:00–4:00							
4:00–5:00							
5:00–6:00							
6:00–7:00							
7:00–8:00							
8:00–9:00							
10:00–11:00							
11:00–12:00							

APPENDIX C
Transcripts for Lectures

Lecture 1 (from Chapter 1, page 21)
Class: Anthropology
Topic: Cross-Cultural Perceptions of Time

Different cultures often have entirely different perceptions of time. The cultural anthropologist Edward T. Hall popularized the idea that cultures use time and view time in very different ways. The idea of the past, present, and future—and the whole concept of scheduling or managing time—can be so different that it leads to cross-cultural miscommunications. In Hall's 1990 book *The Dance of Life*, Hall writes, "Time is one of the fundamental bases on which all cultures rest and around which all activities revolve. Understanding the difference between monochronic time and polychronic time is essential to success."

Hall's notion of monochronism and polychronism can be understood as follows. Monochronic time is linear. Events are scheduled one at a time, one event following another. To a monochronic culture, this type of schedule is valued over interpersonal relationships. On the other hand, polychronic time is characterized by many things happening simultaneously. In addition, interpersonal relationships are highly valued in polychronic cultures.

Hall's theory is that monochronic time can be found primarily in North American and Northern European cultures. These cultures emphasize schedules, punctuality, and preciseness. They also emphasize "doing" things. They are cultures that value productivity, that value getting things done "on time." They view time as something that can be lost, killed, or wasted—or, conversely, they view time as something that can, or should, be managed, planned, and used efficiently.

Polychronic time, on the other hand, can be found primarily in Latin American, African, and Native American cultures. Their perception of time is more connected to natural rhythms. It is connected to the earth, to the seasons. This makes sense when we consider that natural events can occur spontaneously, sporadically, or concurrently. Polychronic cultures view time as being somewhat flexible. Since life isn't so predictable scheduling and being precise simply isn't that important. In addition, relationships with people are valued more than making schedules. There is more value placed on "being" than on "doing."

Different cultural perceptions of time can lead to conflict, especially in the business world. The idea of being late versus on time for a meeting, for example, might differ widely between an American businessperson and a Brazilian; the American businessperson might be far less tolerant of a Brazilian's late arrival. However, the Brazilian businessperson might be offended by an American's insistence on punctuality or on getting right down to business; the Brazilian would generally prefer to finish talking with colleagues first, and would not want to cut a conversation short in order to make an appointment.

Some traditional time management programs used in the business world might not translate well in another culture. Traditional time management programs in the business world emphasize to-do lists and careful scheduling. They are monochronic. However, a business in a polychronic culture might not adjust well to that system. Companies who impose these monochronic systems on places of business in polychronic cultures might be guilty of ethnocentrism, which means making their own ethnic or cultural values central and not valuing other values.

Edward Hall's theory of monochronic and polychronic cultures has been challenged by some critics. Some people think it is overly general. They argue that within any cultural group we might find people who think of time differently. In other words, a primarily polychronic culture might have both monochronic and polychronic types of people. The same diversity among individuals might be found in a primarily monochronic culture. Critics of anthropologists like Edward Hall feel that it's more useful to think of time differences among individuals, not just between cultural groups.

Lecture 2 (from Chapter 2, page 51)
Class: Psychology
Topic: Three Systems of Memory

Psychologists have many theories to explain how we remember information. The most influential theory is that memory works as a kind of storage system, or storehouse, for information. According to this theory, there are three types of these storage systems with different functions that hold information for different amounts of time. These storage systems are sensory memory, short-term memory, and long-term memory.

Sensory memory holds information for the shortest amount of time—less than four seconds. An instant. Sensory memory is where stimuli, or things that stimulate our senses, are very briefly stored. We forget sensory memories almost instantly, unless they pass into another storage system. Examples of stimuli that usually go into sensory memory are things that we see and hear in the world such as a flash of lightning, or the sound of a door closing.

Short-term memory, which is also sometimes called "working memory," holds information for about 15 to 25 seconds. This is not a very long time, but the information that passes into this system has more meaning for us than just sensory stimulation. It is not entirely clear how some sensory memories transfer into more meaningful short-term memories. Some experts believe that sensory information changes into visual images as it is stored, and others believe that information changes into words. However, it has been proven that memory going into this system is made up of "chunks," or groups, of meaningful information (for example, single letters or numbers or more complicated sets of information), and that only around seven "chunks" of information can be stored in short-term memory. Therefore, there is not a lot of room for information in short-term memory, and it does not stay there for very long. Examples of the type of information that typically goes into short-term memory are telephone numbers, addresses, and names.

Long-term memory holds information almost indefinitely, although retrieving it can sometimes be difficult. Think of long-term memory as a very big library, or even a computer chip, with almost unlimited capacities for storage. Information gets filed, catalogued, and stored. Long-term memory has several different components, or modules, that correspond to separate memory systems in the brain. The main two categories of long-term memory are declarative memory and procedural memory. Declarative memory is where we store factual information, such as names, faces, dates, life events. Procedural memory is where we store memory of skills and habits, like how to ride a bike or how to boil an egg. Within declarative memory, there are smaller categories of memory, or subdivisions—episodic memory and semantic memory. Episodic memory is where we place memories that relate to our personal lives, things we have done or experienced, such as having a car accident, celebrating an important birthday, or graduating from school. Semantic memory is where we organize general knowledge or facts about the world, such as math formulas, spelling rules, and capital cities.

Lecture 3 (for Chapter 3, page 76)
Class: Sociology
Topic: Ingroups and Outgroups

In the last class, we discussed the nature of groups: how they are formed, and what characteristics they have in common. Today we will focus on two particular types of groups: what sociologists call "ingroups" and "outgroups."

Let's clarify the definitions of each type of group, and then we'll look at some examples.

First of all, what is an ingroup? Most of us are members, on some level, of at least one ingroup. These are people with whom you feel a close attachment or connection, with whom you identify strongly. An example of an ingroup could be a person's family, or a close group of friends. Members of an ingroup may all dress in a similar style, or listen to similar music, or use a similar way of speaking—they may even have their own specialized words for certain things. However, ingroups typically define themselves not just in relation to the members of that group, but in relation to other groups that are different from the ingroup.

These other groups, in contrast to the ingroup, are called outgroups. An outgroup is a group that is viewed from the perspective of an ingroup, often in negative terms. Members of an ingroup may feel a sense of difference or separateness from the outgroup. They may feel excluded. They may even feel a strong sense of opposition or conflict with the outgroup—or even hatred. Outgroups help to define ingroups by providing the ingroup with a sense of identity against or in opposition to them. The ingroup may magnify, or emphasize, certain characteristics that make them distinctly different from the outgroup. In other words, one person's ingroup is another person's outgroup. To illustrate, members of a neighborhood gang may wear certain types of clothing to differentiate themselves from rival gangs, or from non-gang members—members of the dominant or mainstream culture. As another example—and an even more extreme one—countries or cultures at war may emphasize their difference from the country they are at war with, in order to increase unity and loyalty in their ingroup. This leads to an "us versus them" mentality, that, in turn, can increase any existing conflict even as it strengthens the ingroup's sense of identity.

Ingroups and outgroups tend to view one another in very separate terms, and they usually have little or no interaction with each other. As a result, these groups don't have a lot of real information or firsthand experience with one another. And as a consequence of the lack of information, they rely heavily on stereotypes and misinformation about each other. The stereotypes then reinforce the ingroup's mistrust of or hatred toward the outgroup.

Indeed, ingroups and outgroups come into conflict most frequently over symbolic representations of the groups: objects or places that hold a great deal of meaning for one group, and that symbolize, or stand for, the group in some way. An obvious example of this can be seen in how one country may seek to destroy a flag, a statue, or a building that represents a country it is at war with. During the conflict in Iraq, for example, a statue of Saddam Hussein was toppled and dragged through the streets as a symbol of an outgroup. Destroying the objects and symbols associated with one group can be a way of imagining that they are destroying the group itself. It's important to clarify, however, that the symbol itself isn't the cause of the conflict—it's the meaning attached to the symbol, a point at which members of an ingroup can express their identity as distinct from the outgroup, and a point at which the ingroup can act out its emotions toward an opposing group.

Lecture 4 (for Chapter 4, page 108)
Class: Philosophy / Ethics
Topic: Social Inventions

How important is it for people to contribute to society in some way? After the tragedy of 9/11, some people have become preoccupied with this question. Tragedies have a way of making people rethink their values and find a new focus. They make people think, on some level, about what a society needs in order to survive. Not just basic needs like food, clothing, and shelter, but deeper needs, relating to the health and values of society. Many people find themselves asking: how can I find more meaning in our society? What can I do to make a difference? For some, these questions may lead to practical decisions; others ask these questions and find themselves setting foot on a more spiritual path.

The notion of doing something to take control of society or of our fate as humans is not something that developed just after 9/11. We might date this impulse back to ancient times, when the Greeks believed that humans were subservient to the gods, and that both gods and humans were powerless under fate. What was fated to happen was going to happen, and there was nothing that they could do about it. However, this way of thinking changed, arguably, with the rise of the great city of Athens. The social critic John Ralston Saul reminds us of how the Greeks constructed both new styles of buildings and new structures of civilization. The Greeks began to believe in the power of ingenuity, or the notion that creative, imaginative thinking could lead to humans' ability to shape their own futures. They could use their own ingenuity, and the tools at hand, to make life better. They did not have to be subject to fate. Their thinking changed, in other words, from a passive approach to an active one.

Perhaps somewhere in the late 20th century we began to lose sight of this active way of thinking. According to John Ralston Saul, the notion of "fate" returned with new faces— globalization, the market, or even technology. People in Western society began to feel powerless in the face of these large, looming forces that were shaping our society for us. Now, in the early 21st century, we may be seeing another change similar to the ones that the Greeks experienced, according to another cultural critic, Jon Spayde. In the wake of 9/11, perceiving a need for significant social change and new values, people who call themselves "social inventors" are trying to take back some control over society's direction once again.

A social inventor is not necessarily a social activist. An activist fights for social change. Nor is a social inventor a social contributor; a social contributor might be someone who supports social causes financially, or emotionally. And finally, a social inventor is not necessarily someone who works in a high-tech industry or invents new technologies and consumer products. A social inventor is different because he or she is using the power of ingenuity, or creative thinking, to come up with ideas for change in certain communities or sections of society. Social inventors have a vision of a better world and create new systems or practices. Their ideas may seem offbeat or impossible. Most social inventors are not famous or wealthy because of their inventions. They are usually quite ordinary people; they may even be people you know. Or we may never know who they are. But some of these creative thinkers have powerfully, and quietly, changed the way we live.

Some examples of social inventions may sound familiar to you. The organization of "Alcoholics Anonymous," a support group for people with addiction to alcohol, was founded in 1935 and has been going strong ever since. This was a social invention because an individual named Bill Smith, himself a recovering alcoholic, came up with a 12-step process for creating personal change. The idea caught on, communities and support groups formed around it, and millions of alcoholics have changed their lives ever since.

Another example of a social invention is the organization Amnesty International, which was founded in 1961. A British lawyer named Peter Benenson wrote an editorial after two Portuguese students were imprisoned for toasting freedom in a café, and the international organization to support human rights began. Now millions of people around the world write letters to protest human rights violations.

Social inventions do not have to be organizations, however. Sometimes they are new designs for neighborhoods or communities, allowing for more interaction among people. Sometimes they are systems, like new ways to help prisoners in jails receive an education or re-enter society. Sometimes they are very simple ideas, examples of new ways of thinking or "thinking outside the box" to solve problems. For example, some movie theatres in Boston and New York have recently started implementing a social invention to solve the problem of babies crying in movie theatres. To accommodate parents with babies, who would like to keep up with current movies, some theatres now offer special "mother's hours," a daytime showing of a film in which they are free to bring babies or young children. The lights are not turned down as low so that they can keep an eye on their children while they watch the movie.

The idea of social inventions or social ingenuity has become so popular in recent years that "Idea Banks" of social inventions have shown up on the World Wide Web, books have been published on the subject, and Institutes have been founded. The Institute for Social Inventions, based in London, connects think tanks and idea banks throughout Europe. It has a website that invites ideas from anyone and that I'll write here on the board: *www.globalideasbank.org*. You can search this website by category to see the types of ideas that ordinary people come up with. Looking at a wide range of them gives you some sense of the extent to which people desire to make a difference in our society and not remain powerless.

Lecture 5 (for Chapter 5, page 139)
Class: Psychology
Topic: Causes and Effects of Stress

Everyone experiences stress on some level every day. Stress, broadly defined, is our response to events that we perceive as threatening or challenging. We may experience different levels of stress depending on the *stressors*, meaning the events or circumstances that cause us to feel stress.

Of course, not everyone perceives the same events or circumstances as stressful; we don't always react the same way to the same stressors. In fact, something that is extremely stressful for one person may be exciting and non-stressful for another. In general, though, stressful events can be classified into three main categories: cataclysmic events, personal stressors, and background stressors. Cataclysmic events are major events that cause stress suddenly, immediately, for a great many people at once. Examples of these are earthquakes, fires, or other disasters. Personal stressors are major life events that create stress. They can include the death of a loved one, a job loss, a divorce, a financial setback, or a geographical move. They are not always events that we would perceive as negative; many "joyful" life events can also cause a great deal of stress. For example, getting engaged or married, acquiring a new family member (through birth or adoption), starting a new job, and even taking a vacation can all be as stressful as "negative" life events. Finally, background stressors—which we can also think of as day-to-day hassles, or minor irritations—can cause stress, particularly when they add up, when we are repeatedly exposed to them. Examples of background stressors are waiting in a long line, getting stuck in a traffic jam, being exposed to noise, experiencing a delay of some sort, or dealing with broken equipment. Examples of chronic background stressors—and the kind that can lead to long-term health problems—include being unhappy with one's job, living environment, marriage, or relationship.

Stress is not something that only exists in our mind. Repeated exposure to stressors has both psychological and biological consequences. When we are exposed to stressors, our adrenal glands secrete certain hormones, and our heart rate and blood pressure rise. We experience a "fight or flight" response, a sense of emergency, where the body prepares to defend itself. This is useful in some situations, especially where we might actually need to defend ourselves. In the long run, though, this activation of what is known as the sympathetic nervous system has negative effects and reduces our capacity to manage stress. When stress hormones are constantly secreted, and the body is continually preparing for emergencies, body tissues such as the heart and blood vessels can begin to deteriorate. The immune system functions less effectively, and reduces our ability to fight off illnesses. Some people who complain of repeated exposure to highly stressful circumstances tend to report the following types of symptoms: aches and pains (headaches and backaches are common), skin rashes, digestive problems, and fatigue.

The General Adaptation Syndrome, or G.A.S., explains the sequence of physiological reactions to stress. There are three phases to G.A.S. The first is the "alarm and mobilization" phase. This is when we first become aware of a stressor. When we respond with alarm, we may feel upset or confused. We may even feel a sense of panic or fear. After that, however, we may begin to mobilize our efforts—in other words, to take action to remove the stressor. For example, if you received a mid-semester report stating that your grades were all very low, you might worry at first, but then you would probably make plans to reverse the situation, to improve your grades. It is during this first phase that the sympathetic nervous system is activated and the body responds with a sense of emergency.

The second phase of G.A.S. is the resistance stage, which occurs if the stressor is not removed. This is the stage when we fight against the stressor or try to cope with the stressor. The attempt to mobilize and remove the source of stress from phase one can result in further stress. For example, if you were studying long hours to try to improve low grades, you might succeed in improving the grades but create more stress in the process.

This can lead to the third G.A.S. phase: exhaustion. In this phrase, if resistance was not successful and stressors still exist, our ability to fight or cope with the stressor diminishes. At this point, symptoms of stress manifest themselves psychologically and biologically. Psychologically, we may become irritable, short-tempered, or unable to focus. There may be a sense of being completely overwhelmed and unable to function. Biologically, our bodies may react with such symptoms as aches and pains, fatigue, or illnesses. Interestingly, the exhaustion phrase may actually be an extreme way of trying to avoid the stressors. The body may be telling us that we need to take a break, that we need to do whatever is necessary to remove ourselves from the stressor.

Lecture 6 (for Chapter 6, page 180)
Class: American History / American Studies
Topic: The American Dream: Myth or Reality?

The term "American dream" is widely used today. But what exactly does this concept mean? Where does the term come from? When we talk about the American dream, *whose* American dream are we describing? Is the American dream the same for all Americans? Has the meaning of the term changed over time? Is the American dream a uniquely American concept?

Questions like these can complicate a seemingly simple term and lead us to an even more important question: is the American dream a myth or a reality today?

The term "American dream" began to be widely used in 1867. The term was used in a famous novel written by Horatio Alger. The novel, *Ragged Dick*, was a "rags to riches" story about a little boy who was orphaned and lived in New York. The boy saved all his pennies, worked very hard, and eventually became rich. The novel sent the message to the American public that anyone could succeed in America if they were honest, worked hard, and showed determination to succeed. No matter what your background, no matter where you were from, no matter if you had no money or no family, hard work and perseverance would always lead to success.

Today, the message from Alger's novel is still a prevalent one in this country. It is still used to define the American dream. A very basic definition of the American dream is that it is the hope of the American people to have a better quality of life and a higher standard of living than their parents. This can mean that each generation hopes for better jobs, or more financial security, or ownership of land or a home.

However, new versions and variations of the American dream have surfaced since Alger's novel was published. For one thing, the basic definition I stated a moment ago—the idea that Americans are always seeking to improve their lifestyle—also suggests that each generation wants more than the previous generation had. Some people would argue that this ever-increasing desire to improve the quality of one's life may have started out on a smaller scale, in the past, but today has led to an out-of-control consumerism and materialism. According to this view, we not only want more than our parents and our grandparents had, but we also want more than our friends, our co-workers, and our neighbors have.

Another, more benign view of the American dream is that it is about the desire to create opportunities for ourselves, usually through hard work. A hallmark of the American dream, some would argue, is the classic "self-starter," the person who starts out with very little in life—little money, few friends, few opportunities—and works hard to make his or her way in the world. A classic example of this type of American dreamer would be former president Abraham Lincoln, who was born in a log cabin, was largely self-educated, and yet worked his way up in the world to eventually become a United States president.

This view of the American dream has also been associated with immigrants and their stories, their quests for a better life in a new country. Americans have long been fascinated by immigrant stories, and many feel great pride about their own families who may have come from other countries, worked very hard, and created a better life for future generations. The immigrant story is most often a narrative of upward mobility. Immigrants, seeing this country as a place of new opportunities and possibilities, play a large role in narratives—both fiction and nonfiction—about pursuing the American dream, and indeed, we could point to many success stories.

The American dream has also, historically, been associated with westward expansion in this country. Throughout most of the 1800s, the notion of the frontier—a vast expanse of largely unclaimed land in the West—symbolized new opportunities and a fresh start to people.

Many a dreamer set off for the West in search of land, jobs, gold, or other opportunities, often with next to nothing in his pocket. Unfortunately, this idea of new opportunities in the West had a negative side. The American West was not unpopulated; Native American Indians already lived there, along with other immigrant groups, and these people were often displaced—or met with violence—if they interfered with the visions or ideas of westward-migrating Americans.

A more recent interpretation of the American dream has to do with equality. Civil rights activists such as Dr. Martin Luther King, Jr., used some of the rhetoric associated with the American dream to urge people to work for equal opportunities for all Americans, not just some Americans. A harsh reality was becoming clear to some people, especially in the 1960s and 1970s: not everyone had the same opportunities. If people were denied jobs, education, or other opportunities because of their race, ethnic background, or gender, was the American dream only a myth?

Sample Student Notes from Lectures

The notes in this section are samples of how students might take notes on each of the lectures. You can compare your lecture notes to these. You can also rewrite them to practice using different note review formats, such as the Cornell note-taking method (Chapter 5) and a numeric outline format (Chapter 6).

From Chapter 1: Cross-Cultural Perceptions of Time (Lecture 1)

Diff. cultures have diff. perceptions of time

Edward T. Hall, anthropologist: theory that diff. cultures use / view time differently

- views of past, present, future

- concept of sched./manage time

- cross-cultural misunderstandings

Monochronic vs. Polychronic

- Monochronic: linear, events, sched. One at a time, valued over personal rel.

    North American, European

    Punctuality, preciseness, productivity, DOING

    Time can be lost, killed, wasted, managed, planned

- Polychronic: many things at once, relationships valued

    Latin American, African, Native American

    Conn. To nature, rhythms, earth, seasons

    Time flexible, life not predictable

    Relationships valued; BEING not doing

Time conflicts

- Business world—Americans vs. Brazilians (ex.) and lateness

- Trad. time mgmt. programs: to do lists, monochronic—may not work in poly. Culture

- ETHNOCENTRICISM—making your own cultural values central

Hall's theory of mono vs. poly and cultural diffs

- Some critics say too general. poly. cult. can have both m's and p's
- More useful to think of time diffs. b/w individuals, not just cult. groups

From Chapter 2: Three Systems of Memory (Lecture 2)

Memory as storehouse system, 3 types:

- Sensory memory
- Short term mem.
- Long term mem.

Sensory

- Holds info for shortest amt. Time—less than 4 sec.
- Stimuli (things that stimulate senses) stored
- Things we see & hear in world—lightning, door

Short term (working) memory

- Holds info 15–25 sec
- More meaningful info stored
- How sens. mem. moves into short term? Info changes into images or words?
- Chunks / groups of meaningful info, letters and numbers—7 only?
- Tel. #'s, addresses, names

Long term mem.

- Holds indefinitely but retrieval hard
- Components / modules:

    DECLARATIVE

        Factual info, names, faces, dates, life events

    PROCEDURAL

        Skills, habits

    2 subdiv. Of declarative: episodic, semantic

        EPISODIC—Mem. related to personal lives, what we've done

        SEMANTIC—organize gen. knowledge, facts, math formulas, cap. cities etc.

From Chapter 3: Ingroups and Outgroups (Lecture 3)

2 types groups: ingroups, outgroups

INGROUPS

- Feel close attachmt. To / identify w/ others in grp (ex: family, close friends . . .)
- Members may dress or speak same way, same music?
- Defined in relation to other groups

OUTGROUPS

- Viewed from perspective of ingrp, usu. Negatively
- May feel excluded, in conflict, hatred (rel. to other groups)
- Outgroups help give ingroups sense of identity

INGROUPS / OUTGROUPS & CONFLICT

- Ingroup may magnify things that separate them from outgroup
- Ex: gang members, countries at war
- "us vs. them" mentality
- Lack of exp. And firsthand info—rely a lot on stereotypes
- Ingroups' mistrust of or hatred toward outgroups
- Symbolic representations of grps (flags, statues, bldgs)—meaning attached

From Chapter 4: Social Inventions (Lecture 4)

Imp. of contributing to society?

Tragedies, 9/11—people ask what society needs—health, values

Q. of finding more meaning & making a diff.

    Practical decisions?

    Spiritual path?

History of finding meaning / making change in society

- Greeks

  —believed gods and humans powerless under fate

  —rise of Athens, change of thinking

  —John Ralston Saul— "power of ingenuity" —creative thinking— Greeks felt power to shape own future, make life better

  —passive→ACTIVE approach

- Late 20ᵗʰ C

  —lose sight of active approach

  —new "fate" —globalization, corporations—shape society— feel powerless

- Today / early 21ˢᵗ C

  —back to active thinking? (Jon Spayde)

  —social inventors trying to take back control, power over "fate"

SOCIAL INVENTORS

- Not social activists, social contrib., or high-tech inventors
- Use power of ingenuity to create change—communities
- Offbeat / impossible ideas
- Ordinary people, not usu. famous
- Powerful, quiet change

SOCIAL INVENTIONS

- AA organization, 1935, Bill Smith—recovering alcoholic—came up w/ 12 step process

- Amnesty Internat'l, 1961, Peter Beniston (sp?), brit. Lawyer—wrote letter—now internat'l org. to support human rights

- Inventions can be new designs, neighborhoods, systems, ways of thinking, solving probs.

POPULARITY OF SOCIAL INVENTIONS

- Idea banks on web, books, institutes

- Institute for Social Inventions

- www.globalideasbank.org—can search by category

From Chapter 5: Causes and Effects of Stress (Lecture 5)

Stress: our response to events we see as threatening / challenging

Diff. levels of stress, dep. on STRESSORS (also diff. perceptions and reactions)

3 MAIN CATEGORIES OF STRESS

- cataclysmic—sudden disasters, earthquakes, fires, etc.

- personal—major life events—death of loved ones, divorce, wedding, move, etc.

- background—daily hassles, irritants—can add up—waiting in lines, traffic jam, noise, delay, broken (also CHRONIC—unhappy w/ job, home, relationship)

Repeated exposure to stress: emotional and BIOLOGICAL responses

- adrenal glands

- heart rate / blood pressure rise

- fight or flight

- sympathetic nervous system

- stress hormones, prep. for emergency

- tissues deteriorate

- immune system poor

- symptoms: aches, pains, rashes, digestive probs

GAS: GENERAL ADAPTATION SYSTEM

3 phases:

- Alarm / mobilization phase: 1st aware of stressor—upset, confused, panic, fear—take actions to remove (MOBILIZE) stressor

- Resistant stage: if stress not removed; fight against or coping w/ stressor (stage 1) can cause more stress

- Exhaustion stage: ability to fight/cope less.

    Psych. And bio. Symptoms:

       Psych: irritable, can't focus, overwhelmed

       Bio: aches, pains, fatigue, illness—body telling us to remove stressor?

From Chapter 6: The American Dream: Myth or Reality? (Lecture 6)

"Am. Dream" —q's can complicate term.

Myth or reality today?

MEANINGS OF TERM:

- 1867: term first widely used

    —Horatio Alger, "Ragged Dick" (novel)

    —rags to riches story, orphan boy saved, worked, became rich

    —book sent msg. that anyone could succeed—if honest, worked hard, determined, no matter background

- Basic definition today: hope of the Am. people to have a better quality of life than parents—each generation hopes for better jobs, land, home?

- New versions of Am. Drm. since Alger:

    —consumerism, materialism? We want more than family, neighbors, friends, etc.

    —self starter idea, new opportunities for self—Abe Lincoln, start w/ nothing . . .

    —immigrant story—quest for new life—pride—upward mobil-ity—US a place of new opportunities

    —Assoc. w/ westward expansion, frontier—land symbol. New opportunities & fresh start (esp. 1700s, 1800s) —but neg. side—native Americans and others displaced

    —More recent: equality (1960s, 1970s) —civil rights ac-tivists, ML King—if not everyone has same opportunities (race, sex, etc.), is Am. Drm a myth?

Glossary

Numbers in parentheses refer to the chapter(s) in which each term appears.

abbreviation: a short version of a word (4)

adjective: a word that describe a noun (1)

adverb: a word that describes a verb or adjective (1)

alternative views: opinions of people who may have different perspectives from you, but who aren't necessarily in opposition to you (6)

anecdote: a brief story, which can be used as support for a topic sentence and as a way to develop a paragraph (7)

antonym: a word with the opposite meaning or a contrasting meaning (2)

auditory learning style: learning through hearing (2)

bar graph: a graph with vertical and horizontal lines and shaded bars that can be used to show statistics, such as percentages for different categories; it can be useful as a visual aid in a presentation or a report (5)

body (of an essay): consists of at least three well-developed paragraphs, each of which clearly relates to the thesis (7)

brainstorming: a prewriting strategy that involves thinking about a topic and writing down anything that comes to mind about it (1)

cause-and-effect flowchart: a graphic organizer that shows a sequence of causes and effects of something or a process by which something happens (4)

citation: basic information about an outside source referred to in a text, which may include the title, author, publication date, and page numbers (2)

clustering: a prewriting strategy that involves writing down ideas about a topic and grouping related ideas, usually connecting them with circles and lines (2)

coherence: term used to indicate that the sentences and ideas in a paragraph flow smoothly or fit together clearly (7)

compare: focus on similarities (5)

concluding statement: the final sentence of a paragraph, often a comment on or analysis of the examples in a paragraph (7)

conclusion (to an essay): gives the essay a sense of closure by restating the thesis statement in a new way and summarizing main points (7)

contrast: focus on differences (5)

Cornell note-taking method: a system of formatting and reviewing notes that involves writing comments about the notes in the left margin of a page and a summary of the main ideas at the bottom

course schedule: a week-by-week or day-by-day list of class topics, readings, homework assignments, and due dates of major assignments for a class (1)

describe: give specific details, create a mental picture of something (5)

define: give a meaning or definition of a concept or word (5)

definition signals: words, phrases, or punctuation that may indicate a definition appears near a word in a text (2)

demonstrative adjective: a type of word that refers to a noun and appears before it in a sentence; for example: *this, that, these, those* (6)

development: term used to indicate that the paragraph is of a sufficient length (7)

discuss (in writing): give a detailed answer with supporting reasons/examples (5)

discussion sections (in a class): classes or sections of a class with student discussion rather than lecture from a professor/instructor (1)

distractors: incorrect answer choices meant to distract you from the correct answer; they may use very general language, unfamiliar terms, or ungrammatical structures (2)

draft: a first or early version of a written assignment; this word can be used as both a noun (*write a draft*) and a verb (*draft an essay*) (7)

end comments: a professor/instructor's written feedback appearing at the end of a writing assignment; the comments may be brief or extensive; comments may explain the reasons for a grade or offer advice for revision (8)

enumerate: list examples, points, or reasons (5)

evaluate: write about both positive and negative aspects of a topic (5)

explain (in writing): give a detailed answer with supporting reasons/examples (5)

fact: something that is true (5)

feedback: comments and suggestions, usually about a writing assignment; feedback can be oral or written, and it can come from professors/instructors or from peers (7)

general audience: an audience of readers who are interested in your writing but who may not know the topic as well as you do (3)

grammar log: a list of the types of grammatical errors made in your writing; updated regularly as feedback is received (8)

hierarchical map: shows the relationship of the main ideas to the supporting details, starting with the main ideas (2)

idiom: a word or phrase that has a special meaning that may not be clear from the individual words or a literal definition from a dictionary (5)

illustrate: explain something by providing examples (5)

implied topic sentence: a topic sentence that is not stated directly, but that is understood from ideas or examples in a paragraph (2)

imply: give clues to the meaning of something without directly stating the meaning (6)

infer: guess an implied meaning based on evidence/ideas in a text (also: *make inferences*) (6)

intended audience: a specific person (or people) whom you can easily picture as the audience for your writing (3)

introduction (to an essay): the initial part that introduces the topic and also might try to interest the reader in the topic (7)

jargon: specialized words or terms in a specific profession or academic discipline (4)

journal: a notebook or a section of a notebook (or a computer file) where you can write freely and informally to explore ideas about a topic (7)

kinesthetic learning style: learning through the physical/body (2)

learning style: the way you learn new information (2)

lecture classes: classes where usually the professor/instructor talks and students take notes (1)

margins: the sides of a page that do not contain written text (usually an inch of space on the top, bottom, left, and right); using correct margins is important when formatting a written assignment, and margins of reading assignments can be useful for writing notes (7, 8)

marginal comments: brief comments that a professor/instructor writes in the margins of a paper (8)

narrow (a topic): make a broad or general topic smaller for the appropriate length of a writing assignment (4)

non-verbal language: body language, gestures, and facial expressions that may signal a positive or a negative message about your attitude toward something (6)

noun: a person, place, or thing (1)

numeric outline: an organized system of numbers or letters that shows main points, supporting points, and examples; can be a useful format for reviewing reading or lecture notes, as well as for planning a writing assignment (6)

office hours: times when professors/instructors are available to meet with students and talk about a class or an assignment (3)

opinion: a person's belief, attitude, or value about something; people can agree or disagree with it (5)

opposing views: opinions of people who may have the opposite idea from you (6)

outside source: additional reading to supplement a text (5)

paraphrase: restating ideas from a text using your own words and sentence structures, or "translating" the text into different (simpler) English, usually without reducing the length of the original text (5)

peer review: a process of sharing a draft with classmates (in pairs or in small groups) and receiving feedback (8)

persuasive language: words, phrases, and sentences that present an opinion and try to convince your readers of this opinion (6)

pie chart: a circular graph that can be used to show statistics, such as percentages for different categories; it can be useful as a visual aid in a presentation or a report (3)

plagiarism: the act of representing someone else's ideas as your own, often by using someone else's words without using proper quotation or citation to indicate the source (5)

pronoun: a word that replaces/refers to a noun or a noun phrase and can be used in various positions in a sentence; for example: *he, she, it, they, him, her, them, his, hers, its, theirs* (6)

proofread: a final stage of the writing process that involves carefully going through a revised paper looking for sentence errors/typing mistakes before handing it in (8)

quotation: the use of someone else's words (spoken or from a text) used to prove or explain your point; quotations must always appear inside quotation marks (7)

recite: remember the main ideas of a reading and state the ideas out loud, in your own words (1)

referring words: types of words such as pronouns, demonstrative adjectives, and relative pronouns that connect to words, phrases, or ideas stated in a previous sentence or a previous part of a sentence (6)

referents: nouns or phrases that referring words connect to (6)

relative pronoun: a type of pronoun that begins a relative clause and refers to a specific noun or a noun phrase; for example: *who, whose, which, that, where* (6)

review: look back at notes or questions written after a reading or a lecture (1)

revise: rewrite a draft of a written assignment, usually focusing on content and organization of ideas (7)

revision: a rewritten version of a writing assignment, often with changes made to content or organization (6)

scanning: looking for specific features of a text (1)

seminars: classes with more student discussion than lecture from a professor/instructor (1)

sentence corrections: brief notes or edits, often abbreviations, indicating grammatical, spelling, or typing errors on a writing assignment (8)

skimming: reading text very quickly (1)

source: a text (an article or book) that gives information and viewpoints about a topic

SQ3R System: a reading strategy system that includes five steps: Survey, Question, Read, Recite, Review (1)

subcultures: groups that share in some part of the dominant culture but have their own distinctive values, norms, language, or material culture (3)

suffix: a word ending that tells whether a word is a noun, verb, adjective, or adverb (3)

supporting points or details: specific information (such as descriptive details, facts, anecdotes, and quotations) that help to prove a point and to develop a paragraph (7)

summarize: give an overview of the main ideas (5)

summary: an explanation of the main ideas of a text, using your own words; a summary is usually shorter than the original text because it leaves out details (5)

syllabus: a handout usually given out by a professor/instructor on the first day of class that explains course goals, course policies, and major assignments (1)

synonym: a word with the same or similar meaning (2)

table: a type of graph that organizes information in rows and columns (6)

technical jargon: a type of jargon (specialized terms) seen in texts related to technical fields, such as computer manuals, instructions for technological devices, and articles or textbooks related to the sciences (4)

thesaurus: a book (or website) that gives synonyms and synonymous phrases of words (6)

thesis statement: the controlling idea for an entire essay; it states a clear opinion, or argument, about the topic, and it may also predict the essay's organization (7)

topic sentence: usually the first sentence in a paragraph that states the main idea and possibly a controlling idea or opinion (7)

trace: explain the process of something (5)

unity: term used to indicate that a paragraph is focused only on one topic (7)

verb: an action word (1)

visual aids: pictures, graphs, images, or text that can help an audience follow information in an oral presentation (6)

visual learning style: learning through seeing (2)

visualization: a relaxation strategy that involves imagining yourself successfully going through a process or completing a task (5)

vocabulary log: a regularly updated list of vocabulary words from class discussions and writing assignments, possibly including the sentence where it was found, word forms, the definition, the word used in a new sentence (1)

word collocation: a pair or group of words that regularly appear together and can almost be thought of as one word (5)

writing process: a system of writing that involves at least three steps: planning (or prewriting), drafting, and revising; it may also include additional steps of proofreading and editing to polish a written work (7)